THE IMAGE OF LEADERSHIP FOR WOMEN

Special Edition, 10th Anniversary

THE IMAGE OF LEADERSHIP FOR WOMEN

*How Women Leaders Package Themselves
to Stand Out for All the Right Reasons*

*by
Sylvie di Giusto*

Copyright © 2024 Sylvie di Giusto LLC
All rights reserved

No part of this book may be reproduced in any form or by any electronic or mechanical means, including information storage and retrieval systems, without permission in writing from the author. The only exception is by a reviewer, who may quote short excerpts in a published review.

The information presented herein represents the views of the author as of the date of publication. This book is presented for informational purposes only. Because of the rate at which conditions change, the author reserves the right to alter and update her opinions at any time. Although every attempt has been made to verify the information in this book, the author does not assume any responsibility for errors, inaccuracies, or omissions.

ISBN: 979-8-9901927-1-3

To the glass-ceiling shifters and barrier breakers,
whose strength, foresight, and courage
forge paths in boardrooms and beyond—
shaping a legacy with every step.

Contents

About This Special Edition 9
Foreword by Camille Burns 11
Introduction 17
Chapter 1: Seven Seconds 22
    The Cost of a Poor Professional Imprint 30
Chapter 2: Your Professional Imprint 38
    The Science of First Impressions 45
    The Sustained Imprint 48
    The Invisible Filters of Perception 53
    Stand Out for the Right Reasons 59
    When Details Speak Loudest 62
    The ABCDEs of Your Professional Identity 67
    Internal and External Consistency 71
Chapter 3: Leaders Look Confident 76
    Leaders Are Confident about Their Body 79
    Leaders Are Confident about Their Age 84
    Leaders Are Confident about Their Gender 86
    Leaders Are Confident about Their Style 90
Chapter 4: Leaders Look Authentic 94
    Keywords Are the Keys to Authenticity 96
    The Explorer: Approachable and Relaxed 101
    The Traditionalist: Trustworthy and Reliable 102
    The Cosmopolitan: Sophisticated and Eloquent 103
    The Caregiver: Supportive and Nurturing 106
    The Avant-Garde: Individualistic and Creative 107
    The Glamorous: Magnetic and Extravagant 108
    The Dramatic: Strong and Fearless 110

Chapter 5: Leaders Look Professional 116
   Prescribed Uniformity in Action 122
   Silent Standards and Unwritten Uniforms 124
   Internal Mandates We Self-Enforce 129
   Dressing Beyond the Code: Situational Awareness 137

Chapter 6: Leaders Look Respectful 142
   It's a Sign of Self-Respect 142
   It Shows That You Respect Others 144

Chapter 7: Leaders Look Controlled 150
   Self-Awareness and Self-Reflection 152
   Self-Care and Self-Discipline 153
   Self-Improvement and Self-Promotion 154
   Be Prepared for the Predictable and the Unpredictable 157
   It's Not Only about Clothes 159

Chapter 8: Leadership in a Digital Landscape 164
   KNOW: Assessing the Scope of Your e-Shadow 166
   REPAIR: Correcting Your Cyber Image 169
   OWN: Claiming Your Virtual Real Estate 170
   CONTROL: Commanding Your Digital Boundaries 172
   MONITOR: Persistent Surveillance of Your Online Self 173

Chapter 9: Leaders Lead by Example 176
   The Leader's Challenge: It's Not You, It's Someone Else 178

Chapter 10: Moving Forward 188

Acknowledgments 193

About the Author 195

Perception Audit 197

Your Voice and Our Collective Reach 198

About This Special Edition

Ten years ago, I released The Image of Leadership, not fully grasping the impact it would have on my own career trajectory. At that time, I remember feeling a mix of excitement and nervousness. After all, releasing a book into the world is no small feat. Just a few weeks before I hit that "Publish" button, and while I was still overthinking every single word, Mark Sanborn, a titan of leadership thought and Hall of Fame speaker himself, gave me a piece of advice that has stayed with me: "Nobody cares about your first book, but everybody cares that you have a first book." You know, in the speaking world, a book is an entry point, a business card, a conversation starter—a testament to your thoughts and expertise. So off I went.

That book did indeed open doors and sparked conversations, fulfilling its role perfectly—and much more. But Mark wasn't finished after his original words. He turned around and, while walking off, threw a greater challenge my way: "But you really must write a good second book, Sylvie." So consider this edition my "second good book," the refined version of my initial offering.

You see, a lot has changed in ten years. The digital landscape has evolved rapidly, social media has reshaped our connections, casual work attire has become more accepted, and diversity and inclusion have taken center stage. And we can't forget the profound impact of the pandemic. It was clear that The Image of Leadership needed more than just a touch-up—it needed a full makeover.

The book needed a comprehensive renewal to stay relevant in a world that has fundamentally shifted.

And so I embarked on a journey of complete revision rather than mere superficial changes. This wasn't just about updating; it was about reimagining and realigning the book with the times we live in.

In this process, I made a conscious decision to dedicate several special editions to the incredible individuals I've met and spoken to over the years. You know, as a keynote speaker, the exchange is a two-way street. For every insight I've offered from the stage, I've received an equal measure of wisdom from my audiences. The specific challenges they've shared, the questions they've asked, and the stories they've told have enriched my understanding and approach to leadership. I'm immensely thankful for this reciprocal learning. It's this exchange that has breathed new life into *The Image of Leadership,* transforming it into a special edition that reflects not just my voice but also the collective voice of the many dedicated professionals I've had the honor to engage with.

This special edition is dedicated to women in leadership. It's tailored to address the unique challenges and triumphs you face daily in various professional arenas. It's more than just an update; it's a recommitment to the principles of leadership tailored to the nuances of your experiences—where stakes are high and the demands are varied across industries.

Here's to you, the women leaders, who embody resilience and dedication every day. This book is for you—the ethical, the passionate, the determined. It's a thank-you for your service across fields and a tool to aid your journey forward.

Consider this book the "second" that Mark Sanborn urged me to perfect—a version refined by experience and honed by the passage of time. It's a handbook for the present, a road map for the future, and a testament to the enduring power of a leader's image, transcending the diverse landscapes of all professional sectors.

May this special edition serve you as a beacon through the ever-changing landscape of leadership across all areas of professional endeavor, inspiring you to continue making impactful decisions with confidence, purpose, and authority.

Foreword
by Camille Burns

Over the past 23 years, working with women entrepreneurs, I've witnessed a profound transformation in the landscape of leadership. At the outset of my journey, examples of successful women business owners were scarce, a stark contrast to today's environment where women are gaining the respect and visibility they rightfully deserve. This evolution is not just about increased numbers but a deeper, systemic change in how we understand and appreciate the unique contributions and challenges of women in leadership roles.

To navigate and understand this complex landscape, we turn to experts like Sylvie di Giusto, whose profound insights into leadership and professional identity are captured in this book. Sylvie brings a wealth of experience from a successful corporate career across Europe and North America. As a former head of a management academy and a chief of staff for human resources at Europe's largest tourism and retail group, she developed groundbreaking leadership programs and strategic human resources initiatives. Now an international keynote speaker, Sylvie influences professionals at esteemed organizations such as American Express and Microsoft, utilizing her expertise in the five cornerstones of modern emotional intelligence—visual, behavioral, verbal, digital, and social intelligence. Her approach not only illuminates the path but also guides us through the nuances of building a compelling professional identity.

As women ascend to higher echelons of management and entrepreneurship, they encounter a set of challenges distinctly shaped by gender dynamics. These challenges are not just external, such as breaking through the proverbial glass ceiling, but also internal, involving the psychological interplay of self-perception and societal expectations.

This book dives deep into these dynamics, starting with the critical role of first impressions. Psychological research tells us that these impressions are formed in a blink of an eye, yet their ramifications are long-lasting, influencing opportunities and perceptions in professional settings. For women leaders, managing these impressions is a strategic endeavor that extends beyond mere appearance to embody the essence of their leadership identity.

Confidence, a cornerstone of effective leadership, often carries different connotations when displayed by men versus women. Women leaders frequently navigate a delicate balance—too much confidence can be perceived as arrogance, too little as incompetence. This book explores how women can cultivate a confidence that transcends these stereotypes, a confidence rooted in competence, empathy, and authority that inspires trust and admiration rather than skepticism.

Authenticity in leadership is another dimension rigorously examined here. It goes beyond the simplistic notion of "being oneself" to a more sophisticated harmony between one's core values and their professional persona. Authentic leadership for women involves negotiating the expectations of various stakeholders while staying true to one's identity, a dynamic that encompasses ethical leadership, emotional intelligence, and transparency. This nuanced approach allows women leaders to be true to themselves while effectively navigating the complex landscapes of modern organizations.

Moreover, the influence of cultural differences on leadership styles and professional appearance cannot be understated.

In a globalized business environment, cultural norms shape not only how leaders are perceived but also how they must adapt and present themselves to be effective across diverse contexts. This book provides insights into how women leaders can adeptly manage these cultural variations, turning potential barriers into bridges for communication and understanding.

Throughout this foreword, and echoed in the chapters of this book, the key message is clear: the professional identity of women leaders is not static but a dynamic and strategic construction that involves continuous learning, adaptation, and growth. As we reflect on the journey of women in leadership over the past two decades, it's evident that while significant progress has been made, the road ahead is still filled with opportunities for growth and transformation.

As you delve into the pages that follow, I invite you to consider not just the challenges but also the immense opportunities that lie in redefining leadership. Let this book be both a mirror and a map—reflecting the current landscape of women's leadership and charting a course for future achievements. Here's to the ongoing journey of crafting a professional identity that resonates with power, purpose, and presence.

This book offers a comprehensive exploration of the evolving role of women in leadership. It underscores the importance of crafting a professional identity that not only navigates but also leverages the unique challenges and opportunities faced by women leaders today. Let us continue to inspire, empower, and lead with conviction, ensuring that every layer of our professional identity aligns with the values we champion and the impact we make.

This transformation marks a significant shift from the earlier days when the presence of women in leadership was a novelty rather than a norm. It reflects broader societal changes, where the fight for gender equality has made substantial progress, although challenges remain.

The rise of women in leadership roles coincides with increased recognition of the need for diverse perspectives in decision-making processes that affect economies and communities worldwide.

This change is particularly visible in the realm of entrepreneurship, where women are not only starting businesses at a faster rate than men but are also bringing innovative solutions to the market. Women entrepreneurs are redefining success in business, not solely in terms of financial gain but also in creating inclusive work environments and addressing societal issues.

However, the journey for women leaders is not devoid of hurdles. Access to capital remains a significant barrier, with women entrepreneurs receiving a disproportionately small share of funding. Moreover, women often face skepticism regarding their capabilities and must continually prove their competence in ways that their male counterparts are less likely to experience.

The narrative of women in leadership is also evolving through the lens of intersectionality, where the experiences of women are not seen as monolithic but varied across different races, ethnicities, and backgrounds. This recognition is crucial in understanding the full scope of challenges and opportunities that women face, leading to more targeted and effective strategies to support women in leadership.

Education plays a critical role in this evolution. By empowering women with the necessary skills, knowledge, and networks, we can accelerate their growth and impact in leadership roles. Educational initiatives focused on leadership development, entrepreneurship, and specific industry skills are pivotal in leveling the playing field and preparing women to take on significant roles in business and beyond.

Networking and mentorship are also vital components of success for women leaders. By connecting with peers and seasoned professionals, women can gain insights, guidance, and opportunities that might otherwise be inaccessible. Such relationships are instrumental in navigating the often complex terrain of business and leadership.

The narrative of women in leadership continues to inspire and evolve. It's a story of resilience, innovation, and progress. As more women ascend to positions of power and influence, they not only reshape the landscape of their respective fields but also pave the way for future generations to come.

The significance of these changes extends beyond individual achievements to influence broader cultural shifts towards greater equality and justice in society.

With every woman who breaks the glass ceiling, we redefine what is possible, not just for women in leadership but for all who have been marginalized. This journey is a testament to the strength, creativity, and perseverance of women who dare to lead, innovate, and inspire. Let us carry forward this legacy with unwavering commitment and vision, championing a world where leadership is diverse, equitable, and inclusive.

This book provides a deeper exploration into the themes discussed, providing readers with both inspiration and practical guidance on navigating the evolving landscape of women's leadership. As we move forward, let us remain steadfast in our efforts to support and elevate women at all levels of leadership, recognizing the profound impact they have on our world.

Camille Burns
CEO
Women Presidents Organization

Introduction

Welcome to *The Image of Leadership for Women*. The title reflects the reality that every woman can and should acknowledge, which is that true leadership manifests itself in ways that are both seen and unseen. They're equally important. Even though all leaders have their own individual styles and personalities, it cannot be doubted that the most effective leaders who succeed over a long period of time are seen and accepted because their interior skills and exterior images are in perfect alignment. In other words, what you see is what you get. As leaders, they're consistent and dependable, and their professional imprint—which I'll introduce to you later in the book—is strong and durable. Whether you are masterfully navigating the intricate corridors of a corporate skyscraper, advocating for public needs within the realms of government offices, enriching inquisitive minds in the education sector, driving transformative initiatives in the world of nonprofits, or boldly pioneering innovative ventures as an entrepreneur, you may wonder, is this book for me?

My answer is that this book is definitely for you. It's crafted not only for the seasoned executive or the aspiring leader but also for those who find themselves in male-dominated industries, where the gender dynamics at play present a unique set of challenges and opportunities. Regardless of the landscape—whether you stand as a solitary figure in a boardroom or as part of a growing legion of women leaders—this book is a beacon for your journey, illuminating the ways you can solidify your presence and shape your leadership narrative. It's designed to instill a culture of professionalism and leadership at every level.

The principles laid out here hold true across all levels of leadership because advancement is a constant pursuit, whether you're a seasoned leader aiming for a top executive position, a mid-level professional eyeing a strategic leap into senior management, or starting your leadership journey with aspirations for a pivotal role. As a woman in the workplace, you must proactively cultivate and embody the qualities of these roles well in advance, often navigating unique challenges and carving out your path.

Being recognized as having "leadership potential," as someone who is equipped to manage the upcoming tier of responsibilities and challenges, is essential. It's like an experienced professional in any field setting their sights on a major promotion, or a mid-level manager aiming for the C-suite. The dynamics might differ—navigating the complexities of corporate ladders, mastering the unspoken codes of office politics, or pioneering your own start-up. Yet, the core principle remains the same: no matter if you're at the threshold of your career or you're a seasoned professional making pivotal decisions, the way you present yourself should consistently reflect the leader you aspire to be.

The high-stakes negotiations in the boardroom, the pivotal discussions within team meetings, the charged atmosphere of major project launches, or the strategic choices made in the executive suite—all these scenarios demand leaders who possess not only the expertise but also the professional gravitas to instill confidence and instigate change.

This book will take you step by step through the development of your professional identity. The focus will be on all those things that people perceive about you, with an emphasis on your appearance and your image of leadership. I mean your image as you lead a team meeting, speak at a professional conference, or articulate your vision in an interview. It's based on the proven concept that you cannot simply tell others that you're a leader and expect them to treat you as one. You have to show people your leadership, every day, consistently, and in a way that encourages them to instantly accept you as someone in whom they will place their trust.

We'll begin with the seven-second rule. This is that critical moment when others first encounter you. They may have some prior knowledge of you, but this is the first time they actually lay eyes on you. I'll show you how people make up their minds very quickly about your leadership potential and either open the door for you or slam it shut. The good thing is that this process is entirely under your control. Already within these first micro moments, you can choose to present yourself as a leader or not.

Hence, I'll reveal the components of your professional imprint and how, after it's been established in those first seconds, you need to sustain it over time. We'll explore the ABCDEs of your professional imprint: appearance, behavior, communication, digital footprint, and environment.

Although how you dress is very important, this is not a how-to book or fashion guide. I'm not going to detail specific items of clothing or accessories you need to buy or wear. What I want to provide for you is a deep understanding of the concepts you need to put into practice in your own way. I want to give you the power to create your own professional imprint that is true to your personality, that works for you for the duration of your career, and that also stands as a testament to the organization you're a part of and, by extension, the industry your work in as a whole.

In crafting this book, it was important to me to recognize that women's experiences and identities are vast and diverse. This book is committed to embracing every woman—those who entered this world as women and those who have proudly navigated their journey into womanhood. It acknowledges the breadth of what it means to be a woman in the professional world, encompassing those who have always identified as such and those who have courageously defined their identity at different stages of life.

However, in all my books, I take great pride and importance in using inclusive language. Because this book is directed toward women, I've made a conscious choice to use "she/her/hers" pronouns for simplicity's sake, without excluding those who may identify differently.

Here, every woman is welcome and valued. And it doesn't stop there; perhaps even some of our male counterparts may find this book in their hands, seeking to better understand the specific challenges their managers, team members, partners, or daughters might face.

Although this book is crafted from a woman's perspective, it is not meant to foster division or promote an extreme, radical viewpoint. In my vision of leadership, the intrinsic qualities that make an effective leader are not gender-specific—they are universal. Yet, there's no denying that different environments come with distinct challenges. Although we will explore some of these that are specific to women, this recognition does not negate the adversities faced by our male counterparts.

My hope is that as we continue to progress as a society, we will collectively support and recognize the capabilities of women, ensuring that they stand on equal footing.

Ideally, by the twentieth or thirtieth anniversary of this book, the need for a specific edition focused on women's leadership will no longer exist. By then, all people of all genders will hopefully experience a professional landscape replete with equity, one where leadership is purely about ability and integrity and uninfluenced by gender.

Leaders come in all genders, shapes, sizes, ages, styles, and levels—including yours! I hope this book will help you develop your professional identity on your journey of becoming the leader you deserve to be. It's all a matter of letting people see your inner star that is ready to shine.

Let's get started on this exciting journey to achieving your full leadership potential.

Love,
Sylvie

Chapter 1
Seven Seconds

Seven Seconds:
Just a Glimpse, but the Vision Lasts.
2 3 4 5 6 7

Chapter 1: Seven Seconds

Appearance matters. Every hour of every day, we humans evaluate our environment based on what we see and hear. We avoid situations and people that seem threatening. We gravitate toward situations and people that appear welcoming. When we meet someone, we use sensory information to quickly determine if we're going to get along with them or if we need to keep our distance. We turn on the television and say, "This show looks good. I think I'll watch it." At the store, we inspect the food we want to buy. When a dog approaches us on the street, before we extend our hand we examine its body language. Is the tail wagging or is the dog tense?

Just as we judge others, we're judged by the people who meet us or see us. Do we appear trustworthy? Confident? Or do we appear uncertain or detached? People whom we meet make quick decisions about us. Should they hire us? Vote for us? Buy something from us?

Anyone who aspires to a position of leadership in any capacity needs to understand the power of image. The good news is that your image of leadership is something you can control. You can make it what you want. It's a combination of how you appear, how you behave, how you communicate online and offline, and how you operate within your environment. These are all things you can shape to work in your favor and help you rise to the level of leadership to which you aspire.

Let's start with a story. It's about two professionals, Susan and Kendra, who are aiming for a key leadership position within a corporate setting. They're competing for the role of marketing director at a prestigious Fortune 500 company—a step that represents a major advancement in their respective careers.

Although the story revolves around getting hired, the principles revealed in the story are true across any situation: whether it's a marketer seeking to elevate a brand's presence, an analyst aspiring for a managerial position, or a consultant pitching to a major client.

First, let's meet Susan. Brimming with the anticipation of securing the role, she waits in the sleek lobby of the company's main building. Peter, the chief of marketing, arrives to greet her. With a confident smile that's both friendly and businesslike, he shakes her hand with a firm grip before leading her toward his office.

As they walk through the open-concept office, past clusters of focused team members and dynamic digital displays, there's a thoughtful, yet uncomfortable, silence between Susan and Peter. Upon arriving at his glass-walled office, Peter gestures for Susan to take a seat. He then moves to his side of the desk, and with a brief smile, he scans her résumé. His questions are straightforward. His inquiries are pointed, delving into her past campaigns and exploring the distinctive skills she would bring to the team.

During the interview, Susan has an uneasy feeling. She doesn't think she's connecting with Peter. Her credentials are solid—her résumé is what secured her this invitation—but she senses Peter is seeking something more—or something else. She feels the opportunity slipping away, like water through her fingers. She can't quite pinpoint the issue. Maybe, she speculates, Peter is simply methodical and reserved by nature. After all, assessing marketing professionals is part of his routine, and maybe he prefers to keep an objective stance, affording each candidate the same detached appraisal.

After twenty minutes, Peter closes Susan's file and looks up. "Well then, do you have any questions for me?"

Susan has a multitude of questions, but Peter's composed demeanor has thrown her off balance. She hesitates, then replies that she has no questions at the moment before inquiring about the next steps.

"As I'm sure you will understand," Peter says, "we have a significant number of candidates for this role. This initial interview is just the start of the process. We'll be in touch by next week. Thank you for coming in and for showing interest in the position."

He rises and shows Susan to the door. As Susan walks out of the sliding doors of the headquarters, she senses she's been hastily ushered out. Her prospects for a callback, she thinks, are not very good.

Now let's see how Kendra does during the same process. On paper, she has the same qualifications as Susan. In fact, her résumé is identical to Susan's.

Just as Susan, Kendra receives a warm reception from Peter in the lobby of the company's main building. His smile is engaging, and with a confident handshake, he welcomes her before they start walking toward his office. Throughout the brief walk across the open-plan office, past teams engaged in their work with the soft hum of discussion in the background, Kendra and Peter initiate a light conversation. "So how long have you been with this organization?" Kendra asks. "Did you have any trouble finding the place?" he asks, followed by an offer: "Would you like a water or coffee before we get started?"

When they reach his office, Peter gestures for Kendra to take a seat while he settles into his own. With a sincere smile and a quick review of her résumé, it's clear that Kendra's experience speaks for itself. Peter then delves into her professional background, asking what fresh perspectives she could bring to the marketing team.

When Kendra brings up a recent marketing campaign that she heard Peter's company is launching, his interest is piqued, and he leans forward attentively, pressing her for details on her strategic approach. Sensing an opportunity to delve deeper, he wonders if she'd be open to discussing this campaign further with the senior marketing manager. Kendra agrees without hesitation. A quick message is sent, and shortly, the senior marketing manager joins them, giving Kendra the chance to display her insight and proficiency directly.

An hour after Kendra's arrival, Peter notes regretfully that he must excuse himself for another commitment but wonders if she is available to continue their conversation next week. Kendra confirms her availability and expresses her appreciation for the engaging discussion.

Stepping out of the company's offices, Kendra feels a surge of confidence. She's established a meaningful rapport with both Peter, the chief of marketing, and the senior marketing manager. And she feels optimistic about the next interview she has scheduled for later in the week. It's with another major player in the industry, a fierce competitor of the company she just interviewed with.

At the marketing leadership meeting the following day, Peter shares his insights about the candidates for the marketing director role. Susan's qualifications are considered first. "No," says Peter decisively. "She doesn't fit the bill. She lacked conviction. I can't picture her as part of our team." Then Kendra's profile comes up. "Very impressive," remarks Peter. "She exudes leadership. She has an energetic presence. I believe if we brought her on board, she'd be impactful right out of the gate."

Susan and Kendra. Two capable professionals with equivalent qualifications. Yet, in the eyes of Peter, one seemed mismatched, the other distinguished.

If you were to ask Peter about what made the difference, he might not directly say it was, for instance, their choice of clothing that set one apart from the other—next to, of course, many other factors. However, in the corporate world, where a professional appearance can reflect an individual's meticulousness and diligence, this might have indeed played a crucial role.

Especially in a field such as marketing that is characterized by creativity, even if she was dressed appropriately, it could have been Susan's unadorned suit (lacking a hint of personal flair) or her conservative accessories (missing a spark of innovation) that didn't imprint upon Peter the image of a vibrant, imaginative force beneath an otherwise unremarkable exterior.

He may not acknowledge that his opinion of Susan was formed from the moment he saw her in the company's lobby, dressed understated, leisurely seated, her posture a little too relaxed, her gaze idly locked on her smartphone, scarcely aware of the activity around her. Her apparent lack of engagement with her surroundings might have inadvertently suggested an absence of the readiness or drive that is prized in the fast-moving world of corporate marketing.

The interview? It might have been just an obligation. A formality. Susan possibly never had a chance. As soon as he could, Peter cut the interview short and showed her the door. Despite Susan's potential, she wasn't given a real chance.

In both recruitment and executive circles, the visual appearance and perception of a candidate or colleague is often an unspoken consideration. Although it may be regarded as trivial and not acknowledged as part of the formal evaluation process, it nonetheless plays a part in decision-making. Furthermore, legal and ethical standards prevent citing appearance as a reason for employment decisions. He can't and won't explicitly say, "We can't bring you into our marketing team because your presentation doesn't align with our expectations." Such a statement would cross professional boundaries and could lead to significant repercussions.

He may also not acknowledge that he possibly already has formed an opinion about the candidates before they even meet, influenced by the credentials and images presented in the applications and online personas of the candidates.

Nonetheless, the reality is that in any environment where professionalism is paramount, the impression made by one's appearance can subtly influence the final decision.

Your appearance matters every single time you engage in professional interactions. In any professional environment, the way you present yourself can significantly influence the perception and confidence levels of your managers, colleagues, team members, clients, and stakeholders. A well-curated appearance sends a message of competence and dependability, establishing trust from the moment you step into a room. It's not just about looking good; it's about demonstrating respect for your role and the people you do business with.

Whether it's ensuring your look of leadership is impeccable and reflects your individuality, showcasing something visually that speaks to your creative thinking, or carrying yourself with the poise and confidence befitting your position, every element adds to the overall impression. Each detail of your presentation speaks loudly and can be as pivotal to client relations and team morale as the strategic insights or decisions you contribute.

Everyone knows the old saying "You can't judge a book by its cover."

Yet the hard reality is that every day, in countless workplace interactions, women are judged by their "covers"—whether it's power suits in boardrooms, business casual in client meetings, statement accessories that add a touch of personality, meticulous makeup that highlights your facial features, or even the style and condition of your shoes.

It may not be fair, but it's an intrinsic human instinct. Although we encourage looking beyond the surface, there often isn't enough time for others to form opinions based on deep observation. That's why the brain defaults to the path of least resistance, the most straightforward route for gathering information—through our eyes.

Humans are, after all, visual creatures.

Research led by Doug Vogel at the University of Arizona illuminated the speed at which our brains process images—60,000 times faster than text—and asserted that 90 percent of information is transmitted visually.

Further emphasizing the predominance of visual information, Dr. Mary Potter from MIT led a study that found the human brain can process images seen for as little as thirteen milliseconds. This rapid processing suggests our brains are constantly working to understand the visual world around us. These astounding facts highlight the immediate impact of visual cues on our perception, making your appearance a powerful communication tool.

A woman's appearance is not merely superficial but an integral part of their professional imprint and how they're perceived in those critical first moments of interaction.

Susan might have believed her monochromatic attire was neutral enough to be acceptable based on her past experiences. However, the moment Peter observed her, his internal judgment was clear-cut. He might have thought, "This candidate doesn't grasp the essence of our brand's identity. And I don't have time to teach her."

Of course, it's absolutely possible that in a different company, at another marketing department, or for another chief of marketing position, Susan's attire or demeanor would not have been a pivotal factor. However, for Peter's standards and the particular marketing role she sought, it was not a fit.

The goal is to reflect an understanding of the environment you wish to join and show you can seamlessly integrate into the professional culture of the organization.

As for Kendra, the moment Peter saw her—even before they shook hands—he knew she was a contender. Her outfit, the style of her hair, her choice of accessories, her impeccable shoes—all were indicative of a woman who viewed herself as a leader. And not just any leader, but one who could resonate with the innovative spirit of a marketing environment.

It might have been her creative flair in selecting clothes that broke the monotony, her unique way of marrying classic style with a modern twist, or her special knack for choosing accessories that hinted at a bold, strategic mind. We'll never know for certain. But something sparked in Peter, a realization that she truly "gets it."

Yet, it wasn't vanity that dictated Kendra's look. Far from being an overly glossy figurehead, her visual appearance stemmed from self-assurance. Her composed alertness set the stage. Standing tall and alert in the waiting area, she projected readiness and anticipation for the interview.

When Peter approached, Kendra's smile was wide, authentic—a silent yet powerful introduction. She stepped forward, extending her hand first, ensuring a handshake that was confident and steady.

Every micro-expression and gesture, from her steady eye contact to the assertive stance, communicated leadership. These subtle cues, frequently unnoticed, were the threads weaving a significant impression upon Peter. Kendra's outward presentation reflected her internal preparedness, a synchrony that Peter keenly observed. It was the finesse that transformed a prospect into a serious candidate.

Kendra aimed to present as successful, but more critically, she wanted to be recognized as someone who could seamlessly integrate into the company's ethos. She hoped Peter would see past her attire and acknowledge her potential to contribute meaningfully. She aspired to render her appearance inconsequential—to be trusted immediately and seen as capable of excellence. Kendra aimed to personify leadership, not through ostentation but through an aura of confidence that could galvanize a team to new heights.

The Cost of a Poor Professional Imprint

Although it's your duty to maintain a positive professional identity, it's understood that perfection is unattainable, and everyone, even those in the highest echelons of their field, is prone to missteps. Some errors may go unnoticed, but others could become widely known, perhaps through a viral social media post. It could be a lapse in decorum at a company gala, an inadvertently shared comment that doesn't sit well publicly, or a day when your visual appearance might not meet the expected standards of your role. Not upholding the highest professional standards in every aspect of your work can result in significant consequences such as the following:

- **Diminished credibility:** A woman's appearance may unfairly influence others' perceptions, potentially leading to a decrease in her perceived credibility and authority.

- **Loss of respect from peers:** Colleagues may struggle to respect leaders who do not consistently present themselves at their best, affecting team dynamics and performance.

- **Distraction from leadership objectives:** A distracting appearance can draw attention away from a leader's strategic goals and the primary focus of driving organizational success.

- **Harmful stereotypes:** Wardrobe choices can reinforce negative gender stereotypes, which may impact a woman's progression in her career.

- **Missed promotions:** Failing to present a professional identity may result in being overlooked for promotions or special assignments, limiting career growth.

- **Financial consequences:** Professionalism, or the lack thereof, can influence client retention and business outcomes, directly affecting the organization's bottom line, as well as your financial income.

- **Erosion of personal brand:** A woman's personal brand is essential for her career trajectory. Inconsistencies in professional presentation can erode your carefully built image of leadership.

- **Public image risks:** A lapse in professionalism can quickly become amplified in the media, social media, or public forums, damaging your reputation and your organization's.

- **Undermining of professional boundaries:** Inappropriate attire can blur the lines of professional boundaries, increasing the risk of misinterpretation or misconduct.

- **Workplace hostility:** A lack of professionalism can contribute to an environment where disrespect or bullying may thrive, affecting morale and workplace culture.

You think this sounds far-fetched? Think again.

Yes, when we reflect on the journey toward greater inclusivity in the professional world, we should recognize that overly rigid rules and stereotypes regarding one's appearance have significantly evolved. Luckily, gone are the days when dress codes were stringently enforced without regard to individual expression. Yet still, it often took and still takes a public outrage to eliminate roadblocks.

A notable consulting firm faced a public outcry after sending a receptionist home for not wearing heels. The same firm made it into the press and even to the Supreme Court for denying a capable accountant partnership ranks after being told she doesn't appear feminine enough for this role.

A prominent retail clothing company had to overhaul their policies about employee looks on the sales floor after considerable public backlash. Flight attendants of an established airline successfully challenged severe weight restrictions with a lawsuit. Or think of the woman whose story went viral on social media for being denied a VP role at a tech company; according to her, it was because the recruiter's feedback pointedly critiqued her for not putting "enough effort" into her appearance for a video interview. You might think that recruiter must have been male. Think again.

These incidents collectively remind us that the march toward an unbiased work environment continues. Even if equality is enshrined in law and policy, real-world applications reveal that perceptions of appearance still cast a long shadow over professional evaluation. The journey is far from complete. Even in the most progressive companies, there may be remnants of an unspoken code, a relic of the past that quietly influences decisions and outcomes.

Beneath the surface, stereotypes still linger—whispering preferences that can tilt the scales. This underscores a dissonance between policy and practice, a gap where personal interpretation of professional appearance can still unfairly impact a woman's career trajectory.

To date, there's still a pervasive trend to evaluate women more on their aesthetic presentation than their skill set or personal attributes, even when appearance should hold no sway and should not matter at all. However, society, regardless of gender, still often appraises a woman's value through the lens of her physicality—a scrutiny not commonly applied to their male counterparts. And women themselves are not immune to internalizing these standards, often measuring their own worth by their reflection, which can ripple out, impacting their confidence, focus, and overall performance in roles that have no bearing on looks.

Navigating this tightrope of societal expectations can often lead us to pose questions to ourselves that resonate deeply with the struggle for identity in professional spaces.

"Should I wear heels, dress more masculine, wear more or less makeup, style my hair up or let it down, button up or choose softer lines, accessorize boldly or keep it minimal?" These are questions that cross many women's minds, whether occasionally or on a regular basis, as we seek to balance the scales of authenticity and conformity within the bounds of workplace norms. Each choice is like a thread in the tapestry of our professional identity, woven together in hopes of crafting a presence that resonates with both who we are and who we aspire to be in our careers.

Although it may be disheartening that these considerations persistently weigh more heavily on women, research offers concrete evidence that these aspects do carry weight from a scientific standpoint. The influence of self-presentation on professional opportunities and perceptions isn't just anecdotal; it's backed by studies that shed light on the tangible effects of these choices.

Research by sociologists Dalton Conley and Rebecca Glauber illustrates a disheartening link: a woman's increasing weight is often tied to a decrease in both salary and job status, a correlation that men seem to sidestep. Researcher Jaclyn S. Wong, analyzing data from the National Longitudinal Study of Adolescent to Adult Health, also uncovered a financial paradox: women who invest more in their appearance tend to see an increase in their earnings.

Research out of Harvard, Boston University, and the Dana-Farber Cancer Institute reveals another facet—cosmetics. They've found that a touch of makeup can paint perceptions of a woman's competence, likeability, and even her trustworthiness in a more favorable light.

Many of these studies are summarized and discussed in the 2011 book *Beauty Pays: Why Attractive People Are More Successful*, written by Daniel Hamermesh, an economist at the University of Texas in Austin. Hamermesh reviews research that shows attractive people earn an average of 3 or 4 percent more than people with below-average looks. These professionals are also hired sooner, get promotions more quickly, are higher ranking in their companies, and get all kinds of extra benefits.

Why? It turns out more attractive people often bring more money to their companies and are therefore more valuable employees.

And while there's plenty more evidence that a polished appearance can indeed pave the way to higher earnings and stature, researcher Stefanie K. Johnson, for example, introduces a caveat to this narrative. Her studies at the University of Colorado Boulder Leeds School of Business illuminates a less discussed but critical aspect: sometimes, the very appearance that might elevate a woman's status can simultaneously cast doubts on her professional abilities. According to her insights, the very same allure that could seem advantageous may simultaneously lead to being underestimated in capability and qualification.

Specifically, attractive women may face discrimination when applying for jobs perceived as traditionally male roles, an effect described in studies by Madeline Heilman and colleagues at NYU.

All these studies together suggest a complex interplay between perceptions of beauty and professional competence, highlighting the nuanced challenges women face in the workplace based on their appearance. And this book can only scratch the surface—there are dozens of other studies that could be cited, each adding depth to our understanding of this multifaceted issue.

However, what remains true is the common threat that, for women, appearance is a double-edged sword: a tool that can build but also a test that can question. This twist begs us to ponder how women can navigate these waters—leveraging the positives of their appearance while sidestepping the stereotypes that might work against them.

While historical studies and societal awareness have repeatedly highlighted the nuanced interplay between a woman's appearance and her professional journey, the advent of antidiscrimination laws in corporations signifies progress. Yet, our future presents ever-evolving challenges.

The rise of social media stands as the next frontier—reshaping and perhaps intensifying the focus on physical appearance. Amidst this landscape, the crucial question that emerges is how women will redefine their perception in an era where their image is constantly under the social spotlight.

In our highly connected world, a digital footprint has become indelible, and women have to navigate this space with the awareness that their public and private personas are often viewed through a magnifying lens, making the need for digital diligence more crucial than ever. Every woman, every professional, is just one click away from potential reputational impact. This proximity to public exposure means that online actions can have immediate and lasting consequences.

It's not merely the clear-cut social media faux pas we need to be wary of—those that are straightforward and visible for all to see. Beyond the explicit, it's the nuanced and often overlooked judgments that can be most insidious. The daily, seemingly benign interactions that, bit by bit, shape perceptions and can pigeonhole women into narrow stereotypes without their consent, from screen to screen and around the world.

These stereotypes manifest in many ways: a seemingly innocent picture posted online can either perpetuate gender clichés or might be dissected for its executive presence. Fitness posts, meant to inspire, can be applauded as a commitment to health or misunderstood as self-promotion. Personal items displayed in the background in images or during virtual meetings can be seen as a touch of individuality or misread as a lack of professional focus. Online engagement, from the groups you join to the content you like, can all contribute to a digital persona that's constantly scrutinized and slotted into stereotypes, often without direct control or intent.

Is there an easy solution to this problem?

You guessed it, there's no one-size-fits all formula that can easily be applied for navigating this complexity, whether in person or online.

However, the approach I advocate is about redirecting focus within those critical first seconds. The goal is to render your appearance neutral, ensuring it neither detracts nor defines you. Instead, you want the spotlight on your expertise, your insights, and your contributions. It's about mastering the art of subtlety—making sure your appearance is neither a talking point nor a distraction. Your aim should be that your presence—your eloquence, acumen, and ability—commands the room (or your social media feed), not what you're wearing.

When everything is about your experience, your added value, your skills capturing the attention, your appearance becomes an inconsequential backdrop rather than the focal point. Strive to be memorable for your performance, not your style. And although this strategy of course applies to all genders, for women, achieving this may be a steeper climb, reflecting a continued need for greater change in societal expectations and norms.

And, as we strive for this, it's imperative to acknowledge that nobody is perfect, after all. We all have off days. We all are humans. We aren't robots. You're not always going to have those first seconds laid out picture-perfect. You're not always going to choose the right outfit, right attitude, right words. You're not able to consider everyone's mind while scrolling through your social media feed. You're not always going to be confident, prepared, or able to do what's expected of you. However, what you can do is always try your best and realize that an initial impression is just that—a beginning.

Chapter 2
Your Professional Imprint

The Indelible Mark
Etched in Others' Minds.

Chapter 2:
Your Professional Imprint

Let's begin with some clarity on the lingo. Terms abound in this context. Some might refer to it as "executive presence" or "professional image," others might use "professional identity," and there are those who speak of "personal branding." Each term, although distinct, converges on a core principle: the essence of how you present and define yourself in your career.

Yet it's the initial interaction, this "professional imprint," that etches your reputation into the minds of others. It's a moment as brief as it is lasting, that enduring mark you make in the minds of others during those initial fleeting moments, where the ephemeral dance of first impressions sets the stage for the enduring narrative of your professional saga. This professional imprint is more than just a first impression; it's the genesis of your reputation, the spark that ignites the perception of your leadership image, identity, and brand in the workplace.

It's quick and indelible. Some studies suggest it takes three, seven, or eleven seconds, and they delineate different characteristics you're judged on. In my professional work, I've focused on the study that implies it takes place within seven seconds. However, to be honest, the exact length of time doesn't really matter that much.

What matters more is that this happens automatically in our brains—no matter whether we're aware of it, no matter whether we find it fair, and no matter whether, under our shabby clothes, we've the soul of Mother Theresa.

Our professional imprint is a direct reflection of the attention and care we invest in our most valuable asset: ourselves. It's evident in the meticulous choices we make, from the polished shoes that carry us through our endeavors to the precision with which we tailor our clothing, ensuring every line contributes to a leadership image of competence and confidence. It's the thoughtful selection of a workbag, not merely as a container but as a symbol of organization and readiness for whatever the day may bring. Take for example the care we take in choosing eyewear, which not only sharpens our vision but also frames our intent and focus. Each decision, each deliberate act of presentation, weaves together the rich tapestry that becomes our visual narrative, inviting observers to read competence and readiness into our appearance.

Each detail is a thread in the fabric of the impression we weave, not only benefitting our self-image but also enhancing the esteem of the organizations we represent.

Because the reputation of any organization—whether it's a corporate entity, entrepreneurial venture, educational or government organization, or nonprofit organization—is significantly influenced by the appearance and conduct of its representatives. In every sector, from private firms to public service, individuals reflect not just their personal brand but also the ethos of their employer. Whether in a bustling corporate office or a dynamic start-up, every individual, from the front desk to the executive suite, must offer stakeholders the best possible reflection of their professional commitment. After all, employees are the living embodiment of any organization's values and principles.

So, it's imperative that their first interactions, whether with clients, investors, or business partners, set a tone. It's in these first moments that their appearance already becomes pivotal—it is the first tangible demonstration of their adherence to excellence and their pledge to uphold the organization's standards.

Although the story of Susan and Kendra unfolded in a corporate environment, the essence of the so-called seven-second rule is universal.

Whether you're stepping into a high-stakes meeting, engaging in a virtual conference, posting updates on social media, presenting a business proposal, or attending a networking event, your professional imprint is established almost instantly. Changing this first imprint once it's formed is notoriously difficult, and altering it can be an uphill battle. This is because first impressions are anchored in the primal corners of our brain, where quick judgements were once necessary for survival. These initial categorizations, often made subconsciously, are our mind's rapid response to new stimuli, and once they are formed, they become a filter through which all subsequent interactions are assessed.

For example, when Peter initially encountered Susan and unconsciously placed her in the "not suitable" category, changing that snap judgment was nearly impossible. Because said snap judgements is rooted in Peter's cognitive framework, that subconsciously forces him to seek out information that reinforces his initial perception, while often ignoring evidence to the contrary. Her chance to make a positive impact was lost before it truly began.

On the flip side, when Peter met Kendra, her professional presentation immediately pegged her as credible and competent. Instantly, she became a strong contender for her goals. Peter's swift categorization was governed by the same cognitive processes that shaped his earlier judgement. Subconsciously, his brain was now compelled to confirm his initial favorable impression, scanning for evidence to support Kendra's suitability. In this subtle dance of cognition, his brain worked diligently, albeit unknowingly, to validate that Kendra was indeed the exemplary choice for the role at hand.

This is the power of a professional imprint. It is the ambition of every professional—particularly women, who often face more nuanced challenges in this regard—to be seen instantly as competent and capable, maximizing every opportunity to exhibit their leadership potential.

These critical moments of assessment can happen in any professional environment, and such encounters could unfold in numerous settings. Susan might have been a consultant discussing a business strategy, or Kendra could have been an entrepreneur pitching her start-up vision. The context may vary, but the specific situation matters less than the universal truth: within those first crucial seconds, based on their self-presentation, they are categorized as "doubtful" or "promising."

For those first moments, I'm not talking about your DNA. It's not about how tall you are or your body type, although this plays a role, as you will find out later in this book. I'm talking about the countless things you can do—regardless of the qualities bestowed upon you by the vagaries of the genetic lottery—to develop your best qualities (we all have them!) and minimize your liabilities (we all have them too!).

Additionally, your look of leadership shapes not only how you're perceived by others but also how you perceive yourself. Looking the part can significantly enhance your confidence and effectiveness. For women in professional environments, this means choosing clothing that projects confidence, competence, and authenticity, whether you're in the boardroom, participating in a networking event, or conducting virtual meetings. It's about finding that balance between professional standards and personal style that allows you to feel authentic and act with authority.

Our visual appearance influences not just the perception others have of us but also our own mindset, which in turn affects productivity and the quality of our interactions.

In an experiment led by Within Health, it was revealed that individuals typically look into a mirror one to four times a day, whereas some women report doing so more than ten times. Women magnify their mirror image more than men and devote roughly eight minutes per day to discern their top insecurities: weight, acne, and wrinkles.

Men described their reflections using the top three words "unique," "thoughtful," and "handsome," whereas women used the top three descriptors "kind," "fat," and "plain."

This experiment was confined to a physical mirror. Now just imagine the impact of our self-perception due to the digital world of social media and video calls, where our self-viewing can become even more habitual and scrutinizing. In the pixels of social media and virtual conference rooms, our own image often captivates more of our attention than the meeting at hand.

It's not a matter of wearing power suits every day or specialized clothing but finding the proper balance where you feel empowered and can broadcast your professional best.

The clothing choices we make can act as a form of self-expression, offering a visual language that communicates our identity, mood, and confidence level—not just to others but also to ourselves. When a woman puts on clothes that align with her role and that she feels good in, it can create a positive feedback loop: she may feel more assertive, confident, and in control, which can, in turn, elevate her performance and the quality of her interactions.

For many women, the right outfit serves as armor against the world, providing a sense of preparedness for whatever the day may bring. It can also signal to others that she takes her role seriously and commands respect. There's a reason why terms like "power dressing" have emerged; clothing can be empowering.

Research by Hajo Adam and Adam D. Galinsky from Northwestern University has shown that when you dress in a way that you perceive as powerful, you can experience psychological changes that include increased abstract thinking, which is a key component of leadership and strategic thought. This intersection of clothing and psychology is known as *enclothed cognition*, which describes the impact that clothes have on the wearer's psychological processes. Enclothed cognition is a powerful testament to how the external—the clothes we choose and the leadership image we present—intersects with the internal, shaping how we see ourselves and, in turn, how we are perceived as leaders.

Therefore, it's no wonder this concept becomes pivotal in the microseconds during which we make an entrance, be it in a physical room or a virtual meeting space. In these first micro-moments, our visual appearance leaves a swift yet indelible mark, informing others' instantaneous judgments about our capabilities. This initial imprint, a snapshot taken by the observer's mind, sets the stage for all subsequent interactions and opportunities.

Imprinting can be demonstrated easily. When I speak at an event, I usually enter the stage and count out loud to seven, demonstrating how fleeting yet critical this moment in time is for setting the tone of the audience's perception. Then I open up the plethora of decisions they possibly already made about me without knowing anything about my background, skills, knowledge, or the value I bring to the event at this point.

These seven seconds and the research I rely on in my work is based on a study conducted by psychologist Michael Solomon at NYU. It suggests our initial imprint is not based on a single element; instead, it is a composite of at least eleven different elements that people subconsciously judge within those first moments of meeting us. These elements are as follows:

1. Socioeconomic level
2. Education level
3. Competence and honesty, believability, and perceived credibility
4. Sex role identification
5. Level of sophistication
6. Trustworthiness
7. Level of success
8. Ethnicity
9. Religious background
10. Political background
11. Social/sexual/professional desirability

Yet it's imperative to approach this list with a discerning mind. On one enlightening occasion, I had the honor of engaging with Dr. Solomon in a conversation, and he shared a significant point with me: like many scientific findings, the interpretations of his study have been bent to fit various narratives across the internet and by self-proclaimed experts.

It's one of those pervasive myths that human judgment rigidly conforms to this eleven-elements-and-seven-seconds rule. Yet the study never confirmed this assumption and has been taken out of context.

For Peter, for example, while assessing potential team members, certain elements such as sex role identification, ethnicity, religious and political background, and sexual desirability should not influence his judgment and are ethically required to hold no sway in professional evaluations.

However, attributes such as competence, honesty, believability, credibility, and trustworthiness are paramount. Peter's initial assessment of Susan's and Kendra's presentations probably led him to subconsciously categorize them based on critical professional qualities.

In contrast, if you're introduced to a potential romantic partner, the imprint values will be rearranged. In such a situation, their social/sexual/professional desirability will probably leap to the top of the list, along with sex role identification. Should these aspects not align with our expectations, our view of all other attributes might be subtly tinted.

Although one might hope these initial imprints could evolve and change over time, most of us know how challenging it can be to reshape this first opinion. These impressions are the lens through which all subsequent qualities are filtered, and not acknowledging these early signals can lead to difficulties.

The Science of First Impressions

Let me introduce you to one more study on the subject of first impressions. We'll take a close look at how this research was carried out, dissecting each step of the study to fully understand the results and their implications for our daily interactions. However, it's important to remember that this is but a single piece of a larger scientific consensus and cannot be universally applied to every situation precisely as described. It's a reflection of a broad scientific understanding that, even though first impressions can be powerful and enduring, specific outcomes and interpretations may vary depending on context and individual circumstances.

In 2009, neuroscientists at NYU and Harvard identified the neural systems involved in forming first impressions of others. Their study, which shows how we encode social information and then evaluate it in making initial judgments, was conducted in the laboratory of Elizabeth Phelps and reported in the journal *Nature Neuroscience*. The study was based on the concept that each new person whom we meet presents a set of ambiguous and complex information. Because it's a first meeting, the information is primarily visual, although other senses—hearing, smell, and even touch if you shake hands—can come into play.

We quickly sort through this information and judge whether we're attracted to that person or not. It's an ancient and deeply embedded process that allowed our ancestors to quickly assess their relationship to a new person: Friend or foe? Social superior or inferior? And perhaps most significantly, will this person be useful to the group—a leader—or will they be a burden and consume more than they contribute?

But how does this complex process happen? The study sought to investigate the brain mechanisms that give rise to impressions formed immediately after meeting a new person. To explore the process of first impression formation, the researchers designed an experiment in which they examined brain activity when participants made initial evaluations of fictional individuals.

The researchers gave participants written profiles of twenty individuals with different personality traits. The profiles, presented alongside pictures of these fictional individuals, included scenarios indicating both positive (e.g., intelligent) and negative (e.g., lazy) traits in their depictions.

After reading the profiles, the participants were asked to evaluate how much they liked or disliked each profiled individual. These impressions varied depending on how much each participant valued the different positive and negative traits conveyed. For instance, if a participant liked intelligence in a partner more than they disliked laziness, they might form a positive impression of someone.

During this impression formation period, the researchers observed the brain activity of the participants using functional magnetic resonance imaging. Based on the participants' responses, the researchers were able to measure the difference in brain activity when they encountered information that was more important in forming the first impression. During the encoding of impression-relevant information, the neuroimaging results revealed significant activity in two regions of the brain. The first, the posterior cingulate cortex has been linked to making economic decisions and assigning subjective value to rewards.

The second, the amygdala, is a small structure in the medial temporal lobe that has previously been linked to emotional learning about inanimate objects and social evaluations based on trust or race group. In the study, these parts of the brain showed increased activity when encoding information that was consistent with the impression.

The study suggested that when we only briefly encounter others and have limited and ambiguous cues to evaluate, brain regions that are important in emotional learning and value representation are engaged. When encoding everyday social information during a social encounter, these regions sort information based on its personal and subjective significance and summarize it into a single value—that is, a first initial imprint.

Thus, we can formulate the following equation: our emotional learning + our values = the person's imprint. And this imprint is multidimensional, extending its influence far beyond the initial point of contact. It's an intricate interplay of personal and professional signals that collectively shape the narrative of our professional identity. It's not a static or isolated occurrence; it's a dynamic force that echoes across various facets of our professional landscape. It's the subtle yet powerful undercurrent that can sway decisions, alter interactions, and steer the course of our professional journeys. As we unpack the significance of this imprint, let's explore how it reverberates.

Consider the impact on yourself. When you project confidence and competence, you're more likely to feel empowered and capable in your role. This self-assurance can translate into improved performance.

Reflect on your familial and social circle. The way you present yourself professionally not only influences yourself but also extends to the perceptions of your family and social networks. It can establish a halo of trust and respect that permeates your entire support network.

Think about those you interact with. Clients, colleagues, business partners—any stakeholders form their initial impressions of you based on various factors, including your appearance. By presenting yourself in the best possible way, you inspire trust and credibility, fostering stronger relationships and better outcomes.

Acknowledge the organization you represent. Whether you're navigating the corporate world, spearheading your own entrepreneurial endeavors, or collaborating with other professionals in any field, the way you present yourself casts a reflection not just on you but on the organization you're affiliated with.

By embodying high standards of professionalism and integrity, you bolster not only your own leadership image but also that of the collective entity you represent.

Evaluate the industry-wide implications. Your individual identity also casts a wider net, affecting the collective image of the industry you work in as well as the professional community of women in this industry and beyond. This influence can bolster public confidence in women's expertise across various sectors, encouraging a greater societal embrace of women-led businesses, initiatives, and leadership roles.

Therefore, it's essential to be mindful of how you present yourself in every interaction because it can have far-reaching effects.

The Sustained Imprint

Your initial impression is pivotal, yet it's merely the precursor to what must become a deeply rooted perception. Consider this the inception of your "sustained imprint." It's the ongoing cultivation of this first impression that cements your presence and maintains its potency over time. Without nurturing, even the most stellar beginnings can fade, losing their resonance and diminishing their initial influence. Your first imprint is only the beginning. It needs to evolve into a lasting positive impression. I call this the "sustained imprint."

I once developed and organized a leadership seminar for a group of leaders from the retail and tourism company I worked for. The participants were quite surprised to find out their trainer was not a person; instead, we trained them with the help of horses.

In one of the first exercises, we split the participants into two groups. The first group went into the riding area, where an unleashed horse was waiting for them.

The participants were told to walk in straight with confident steps, to appear strong, to keep eye contact with the horse, and to keep a straight face.

When they arrived at the horse, they had to smack their horsewhips on the ground several times. The horse immediately began to run in a circle. The participants whipped and whipped, and they were briefed to stop when the horse appeared to be tired or simply ready for the next step to come.

When they put aside the whip, something rather magical happened: the horse followed them everywhere. Participants walked around the horse arena, and their assigned horse happily trotted after them. None of the participants had said one word to the horse. The horse just followed.

The second group received a different briefing. They were supposed to walk in and appear friendly and kind to the horse. They were told to motivate the horse by petting it, talking to it, and developing a relationship. They even brought in treats and encouraged the horse with all their hearts.

The first observation we made was that they had a really hard time making the horse run in a circle. It was obvious the horse wanted more treats and more tender loving care. Not much happened. The horse didn't follow and at one point didn't even come back for more treats because, obviously, there were no more.

What did we learn? Horses, much like people, respond to the nonverbal cues of confidence and assertiveness. The first group's authoritative approach, conveyed through their posture, gaze, and decisive actions, left a compelling imprint on the horses, commanding respect and prompting a clear behavioral response.

This underscores the power of a strong initial imprint; without uttering a single word, their commanding demeanor set the tone for the interaction, resulting in the horses' compliance and subsequent allegiance.

We then also observed that the first group, emboldened by their initial success, celebrated with a sense of triumph, embodying the spirit of leadership and victory.

However, as time progressed, the complexity of their challenge unfolded. They began to display inconsistency in their demeanor and actions.

To the horse, their once clear and commanding presence became unpredictable. And predictability, along with consistency, is the cornerstone of leadership—it's what engenders trust and respect. We seek reliability in leaders' appearances, words, and decisions and in the steadiness of their conduct.

The first group, although initially successful in commanding attention, failed to uphold the robustness of that initial imprint. They did not succeed in cultivating it into a sustained imprint. The horses' diminishing responses was a clear testament to the group's faltering consistency. The lesson was vivid and unequivocal: a leader's impact is measured not only by the strength of their initial imprint but also by the enduring presence they manage to sustain over time.

The game isn't over after seven seconds. Outstanding leaders leave lasting impressions by how they look and how they present themselves, always and everywhere—consistently. Like Kendra's experience, the positive imprint developed in mere seconds only got her in the door. It made the possibility of acceptance very real. It broke down the barrier between her and Peter. However, the true test of her leadership and her professional identity will be in how she will sustain and built upon that initial approval, proving her value and substance in every subsequent interaction and decision in the near future, and beyond.

Conversely, the negative impression that Susan created caused the door to slam shut. It reduced the possibility of acceptance and created a barrier between her and the person she met—who, in this case, had the power to either help her up the ladder of success or pass her by in favor of someone else. She will never even get the chance to prove her excellence or reveal the depth of her expertise because the brief encounter in the waiting area had already casted a shadow on her interview ahead.

In the glass-walled high rises of corporate powerhouses or the energetic buzz of start-up hubs, whether navigating the structured pathways of government institutions or the collaborative networks of academic circles, even within the mission-driven walls of nonprofits, your initial imprint needs to be confirmed, constantly and every day.

In every setting that calls for your close attention, every interaction and choice contributes to your lasting professional legacy. The warmth of a greeting, the thoughtfulness of an environment, and the focused attention offered to colleagues and clients alike are threads in the tapestry of your enduring reputation. Even outside the confines of your office, your influence extends into the community, whether at industry events or during casual interactions.

You might question whether the continuity of this positive, sustained imprint is solely contingent upon our appearance. Clearly, it's not the sole factor, yet it's significant. Your appearance, throughout the entire process, acts as a critical filter through which all your professional behaviors and communications are perceived. It's a silent but powerful language that precedes and punctuates every action. It sets the stage upon which your competencies are judged. Although not the entire story, it's an essential chapter in the narrative of your professional identity.

There's a famous study by Albert Mehrabian that suggests the words you say—the actual words, not the tone or inflection—account for only 7 percent of the imprint you make. It's called the 7 percent–38 percent–55 percent rule. Words account for 7 percent, tone of voice accounts for 38 percent, and body language accounts for 55 percent of the imprint you make.

One might think (or might have heard) this study suggests it's not important what you say or how you behave; it's only about appearance. Of course, that's just not true. It's another internet myth, and Mehrabian himself made countless attempts to clarify that the study should not be interpreted this way.

Still, countless coaches, trainers, and speakers use this study to suggest the thing that matters most is appearance, neglecting the significance of verbal communication and behavior—and that is just not true.

However, if you have only seven seconds to make an excellent first impression, your appearance takes on greater importance. In those fleeting moments, it's unlikely there will be time to showcase your behavior and communication skills. Think of the countless times you've been in a meeting and someone enters the room—whether they're poised, polished, or disheveled, you instantly form an opinion. Or consider seeing someone on a busy street; their attire, from suits to casual wear, elicits immediate assumptions about their profession or status. Picture yourself scrolling through your social media feed and pausing at a striking new haircut that a friend has posted. Without knowing more, you're already considering whether her stylist might work magic on you too. Or imagine that moment you walk into a boutique and the salesperson's elegant attire persuasively suggest the quality of the store's selection before you've even browsed.

Each day, from a stranger's handbag that catches your eye on the subway, hinting at her taste, to observing a fellow passenger's novel on the plane, silently inferring their interests and perhaps even their personality, we form impressions incessantly. These instances underscore a truth we all navigate—appearance often speaks first, and our brains are intricately wired to listen.

No one is exempt from this instinctive process; it is a fundamental aspect of our human cognition.

You'll recall that Susan and Kendra had identical résumés. (This is not just a hypothetical; in today's competitive job marketplace, among dozens of qualified applicants for a given position, there are bound to be several candidates who look the same on paper.) The chances are good that when Peter first met them and they had a conversation—that is, during the first few seconds—there wasn't much difference in the actual words they spoke.

Those initial moments are simply too fleeting to demonstrate one's verbal prowess. Instead, in such brief encounters, it's our visual and perhaps even our sensed presence that speaks volumes. The human brain, in its quest for instant understanding, relies primarily on the visual cues it receives, complemented by the subtle undercurrents of what it feels rather than what it hears.

As Susan and Kendra awaited their turns in the waiting area, silent narratives unfolded within mere moments of Peter's approach. They cast a long and sometimes indelible shadow, setting a stage where unseen forces came into play. These forces, subtly yet powerfully, influenced the trajectory of Peter's judgments. Like invisible threads, they pulled at the fabric of perception, weaving assumptions and conclusions based on the initial visual encounter. These energies, silent but potent, elevated Kendra in a halo of positive light and shrouded Susan in a cloud of skepticism.

For you, navigating this landscape with awareness and finesse can turn the tide of initial imprints and unconscious judgments in your favor, cementing a reputation that stands resilient and sustains through time.

The Invisible Filters of Perception

Put yourself into the shoes of a patient, for just a moment. You find yourself needing quick medical care, and as you enter a practice, a sea of expectations and anxieties floods your mind. The receptionist is busy typing, not noticing you right away. As seconds tick by—which seem to feel like an eternity—you start to feel a bit ignored.

During that time, your eyes wander, and you can't help but notice the receptionist's nails look like they could use some attention. Their makeup and hair seem a bit much for such an early hour. When they finally do greet you, your patience has worn thin. You were on time, but now they've left you waiting. Finally, sitting down in the waiting room, you spot a crumpled piece of paper under a chair—missed by the cleaners, perhaps.

The chairs around you show signs of age, with cracks and worn edges. Then, as you're called to see the doctor, a strange smell drifts from the staff room. Maybe they just had lunch?

The doctor comes to get you, moving quickly, not stopping for introductions or handshakes. Their shoes have seen better days, and their white coat has lost some of its brightness. All these little things add up in your mind, painting a picture of a place that might not be up to the mark. "No wonder," you think to yourself. "This seems to be the standard in this practice"—a standard that feels lacking.

What you just experienced is the powerful influence of unconscious biases leading your mind to make snap judgments. The sights and impressions, from the receptionist's appearance to the subtle cues of the environment, all funnel through your perceptions, coloring your expectations—possibly even without a word being spoken.

These biases are like silent storytellers, weaving narratives that may not necessarily be accurate or fair. However, they set the stage for your experience, and as we peel back the layers, you'll see how these hidden scripts can shape our interactions and decisions in profound ways. Unconscious biases are mental shortcuts or patterns of thinking that influence perceptions without conscious awareness. These biases are often based on social stereotypes, personal experiences, or cultural norms.

Confirmation bias, for example, is one of the most prominent unconscious biases. Confirmation bias is a psychological phenomenon in which individuals favor information that confirms their preexisting beliefs or hypotheses. It's the tendency to seek out information in a way that validates their existing perceptions. This means we're more likely to notice details that support what we already think, often overlooking evidence to the contrary. From the moment you walked through the door of this practice, your brain was picking up on cues and details that began to form an impression.

When the receptionist didn't immediately look up, their unpolished appearance confirmed any lurking thoughts that the practice is disorganized or unprofessional. Each subsequent observation, from the crumpled paper to the worn furniture to the doctor's hurried entrance, built upon this initial judgment.

Instead of seeing these as isolated instances, confirmation bias led you to interpret them as part of a pattern, reinforcing the belief that the practice does not meet the standards of care you expect. Each detail seems to confirm your initial impression, and this bias can be particularly challenging to overcome once it takes root.

Anchoring bias is another pervasive mental shortcut we often take in which we rely too heavily on the first piece of information we receive about a subject—the *anchor*—and allow it to disproportionately influence our subsequent judgments and decisions.

Once an anchor is set, other interpretations and information, even if more relevant or factual, tend to be viewed through the lens of this initial reference point.

Suppose the initial delay and the receptionist's disheveled appearance were the first bits of information you registered. These details likely became your anchor. As you continued to wait, even before noticing the crumpled paper or the smell from the staff room, your mind was already anchored to the notion that this practice was subpar. This early anchor had an impact on your entire perception of the care provided, regardless of the actual quality of the medical services you received.

The **horn effect** leads you to attribute negative characteristics based on a single perceived flaw, causing you to view all traits of an individual or entity negatively. For example, the receptionist's posture, which could be neutral or simply a product of a long day, might seem to you to indicate a lack of interest or enthusiasm. This bias can lead you to overlook any instances of competence or moments of kindness, focusing instead on these traits that seem to confirm your initial negative impression.

Negativity bias is another cognitive phenomenon in which negative aspects have a more significant impact on an individual's psychological state than do neutral or positive things. Essentially, we tend to pay more attention to, and give more weight to, negative experiences or information.

Did you even notice the receptionist's meticulous uniform? Or what about the effort they put into carefully documenting patient cases, a sign of thoroughness and dedication? Did you observe the efficiency with which they eventually handled your paperwork or the accuracy in their data entry? Similarly, the doctor's speed may have been a reflection of their ability to manage a busy practice effectively, ensuring every patient receives timely care.

However, these positive traits may have been eclipsed by the more immediate negative judgments, steering your overall impression toward the unfavorable due to the negativity bias.

And even after you've left the practice, unconscious biases continue to steer your mind.

Availability bias ensures you overestimate the likelihood or importance of certain events or outcomes based on their ease of recall or availability in memory. This means the negative aspects you noticed loom larger in your memory than the positive ones. They become the ready examples that come to mind when you reflect on your visit or discuss it with others.

This tendency can extend to the point where you might find yourself at home browsing online reviews of the practice, unconsciously searching for further confirmation of your initial opinion. As you skim through numerous positive testimonials, they barely register; instead, your attention zeroes in on the few critical remarks. These resonate with your experience, reinforcing your perspective. Feeling validated, you consider it almost a duty to add your own critique to the mix.

Welcome to the **bandwagon effect** in action—a bias that compels us to adopt beliefs or behaviors because they seem popular or because others are doing it. In this context, the critical comments of others echo your own impressions, and the weight of collective criticism may feel like an undeniable proof, further solidifying your initial judgments.

The **Dunning–Kruger effect** may also take hold as you consider leaving a review. Feeling qualified to evaluate the entire medical staff after a single visit, this bias overstates your own expertise, leading you to assert judgments that might not reflect the true caliber of the health care professionals' skills and services.

The **Sunk cost fallacy** may cause you to persist in viewing the practice negatively because you've already invested in visits and treatments there, despite there being evidence of good care in the future.

I could go on and on. At the moment of writing this book, science is aware of approximately 185 biases that influence the human mind.

These biases work beneath the surface of consciousness and affect every aspect of our lives, from the mundane to the critical, without us even realizing it. Understanding these biases is key to navigating the complex landscape of human thought and perception, allowing us to make more informed and deliberate choices.

And while unconscious biases can have a harmful and pervasive effect—manifesting in serious issues like workplace harassment and obstructing diversity efforts—they can also play a positive role for you in the brief window in which perceptions are formed and professional imprints are made. In this narrow but critical space, you can harness the power of these biases to your advantage.

By being aware of them and intentionally presenting yourself in a manner that aligns positively from the very first moments, you can influence others to see you in a more favorable light along the way. This doesn't mean manipulating perceptions dishonestly but rather ensuring that the genuine and best aspects of your professional identity are what shine through and resonate the most.

For the practice we just visited, if, upon your arrival, the receptionist had briefly looked up and acknowledged you with a smile, making it clear they were wrapping up important work for another patient's care, your impression might have been different. Maybe they could have offered you a glass of water or a cup of coffee while you had to wait. Their unkempt nails maybe would have faded into the background, overshadowed by their meticulous uniform and the courtesy of their instant greeting. You might have thought to yourself, "They're really dedicated to each patient's privacy and care." As you took your seat, the receptionist's professionalism might have cast a positive light on the surroundings, making the waiting room's imperfections seem less significant; instead, you might have noticed the beautiful paintings by a local artist on the wall. When the doctor arrived promptly, their efficient manner could have been seen as a sign of a well-run practice that values your time, turning a potentially negative first impression into a positive reflection of the practice's standards.

However, using unconscious biases to your advantage is not accomplished by making just a good impression; it requires crafting an exceptional one. To stand out in a sea of sameness is to go above and beyond the expected, to offer the unexpected in ways that positively disrupt and dismantle preconceived notions. It's about embodying excellence in every action and interaction and turning the ordinary into the memorable.

The question, then, isn't simply about being noticed—it demands being unforgettable. How can you truly stand out? The answer lies not just in what we do but in how we do it—with intention, with difference, with a touch of the remarkable in the everyday.

Stand Out for the Right Reasons

In the competitive landscape of modern workplaces, where stakes are high and distinction is paramount, standing out is more than a personal goal—it's a professional necessity. Excellence is the new norm across industries, from tech to finance to education to entrepreneurship. Regardless of gender identity, women aiming to lead must transcend the ordinary.

The truth is, "good" doesn't cut it anymore—"good" is the baseline, the expectation. To be perceived as a leader—and to truly make an impact—you can't afford to simply fit the mold. Average blends in, and by blending in, you become invisible.

Think of the game *Tetris* for a moment. For some readers, *Tetris* is a nostalgic nod to the past, a digital relic from the days of clunky, handheld gaming devices. For others, perhaps of a younger generation, it's a classic that's been rediscovered on smartphones and modern gaming platforms. No matter the version you're familiar with, the metaphor stands: each piece that falls is designed to fit perfectly into a space, completing a line. The goal is to rotate and align falling blocks to complete lines.

But what happens when the line is completed? It disappears. This is a triumph in *Tetris*, but in your career, it's a warning. When you align too perfectly with the patterns already in play, you risk becoming part of the background—another completed line that serves its purpose and then vanishes in the sea of sameness.

When leaders stand out, they do so by transcending the ordinary. They become the piece in *Tetris* that not only fits but also starts a reaction, changing the landscape, challenging the status quo, and bringing new possibilities into play. Standing out means being the architect of your perception, crafting your professional identity with intention, and making choices that set the stage for how you're viewed in the professional sphere. It's about proactive distinction—carving out a space where your individuality and unique approach to your career resonate unmistakably.

This requires being the memorable piece that doesn't just fill a gap but also creates a new path for others to follow.

You might be thinking, "Well, is it really always good to stand out?" For a pop star, standing out from the crowd in any way they can will always bring positive returns. Whatever gets their name mentioned in the press will help sell their records. For an entertainer, standing out from the crowd, regardless of the reason, is good to an extent. If they get on the evening news simply because everybody thinks they have done something out of order, they've won the game.

But in the professional universe, standing out for its own sake is a terrible idea. In the professional space, there's a great way to stand out and there's a bad way to stand out.

The surest path to standing out in the best way is to consistently do three things:

- **First, be your very best self,** bringing your unique strengths and personality to the forefront.

- **Second, embody and uphold the highest values of your organization,** serving as a living testament to its mission and principles.

- **And third, don't just meet expectations—surpass them.** Strive to go above and beyond what's anticipated, delivering a performance that's not just good but exceptional.

The bad way to stand out is . . . well, any other way.

It's this commitment to excellence that will distinguish you in any profession.

Imagine, when you walk into a practice, you're greeted not just by a friendly receptionist but also by a wave of innovation. The receptionist, with a welcoming nod, directs you to an interactive kiosk.

It's an engaging check-in experience where you can personalize your visit—choosing room ambience settings from temperature to lighting, right down to the background music. In the waiting area, you're immersed in an environment designed for comfort and education. You instantly notice a refreshment bar—a gesture of hospitality that goes beyond the expected. Here, the receptionist offers a selection of herbal teas and nutritious snacks, transforming the waiting time into a moment of relaxation and nourishment for the body and mind.

In your hands, a tablet becomes a window to new knowledge. With an augmented reality application, you explore health topics in a way that's interactive, immersive, and personalized to your health journey. Posters on the wall spring to life, providing a depth of understanding that pamphlets could never match. Amidst this, a subtle scent fills the air. The receptionist explains it's aromatherapy, intentionally chosen to create an atmosphere of calmness. It's a thoughtful touch that eases the inherent tension of waiting for a medical appointment. Instead of outdated magazines, the area features an exhibition of local artists' works. With art therapy books to peruse, the space is transformed into a sanctuary that indulges your senses and promotes healing.

At every turn, this practice has gone above and beyond. Even feedback is revolutionized; with a real-time device, you can express your level of satisfaction, empowering you as a partner in the care experience. Later in the day, the doctor even personally calls to check on your progress, instead of delegating this task to administrative staff. It's a continuous loop of communication, ensuring your comfort is not just met but treasured.

This practice has redefined what it means to stand out, ensuring that from the moment you walk in to the last farewell, your experience is anything but average.

When Details Speak Loudest

In a world brimming with competence (and competition alike), where "good" has become the standard, the nuances of excellence whisper the secrets of distinction. Leaders who stand out are often those who understand that mastery lies not just in grand gestures but also in the eloquence of details. It's the fine print and the subtleties that can amplify a voice in a symphony of sameness.

The same principle applies to the professional imprint you leave. In your look of leadership, it's the attention to detail that speaks volumes.

It's the crisp dress or the perfectly tailored suit that projects authority, the signature accessory that hints at creativity, or the elegantly simple portfolio that showcases one's work with sophistication. It's the red soles of your heels, subtly peeping from beneath a conference table, that hint at a polished and exclusive choice. It's the well-kept notebook with its neatly aligned edges, whispering of your methodical approach to your work. It's the gentle click of a quality pen, the unspoken ally of your thoughts during meetings, and the smartwatch that discreetly keeps you on schedule, reflecting a blend of modern efficiency and timeless style.

It could be the unique business card that reflects a personal brand or the thoughtful office decor that signals innovation. On a company website, a photograph that captures you engaged in a dynamic team discussion, or mentoring others, sends a powerful message of collaboration. A professional headshot on your LinkedIn profile speaks volumes about how serious you take your role.

These nuances collectively weave the narrative of a woman's commitment to her field and her inherent role as a trailblazer. These are the silent yet potent languages of excellence, the dialects of distinction that resonate with others.

In the same vein, it's the finer details of presentation that can sometimes cause women to stand out—and be remembered—for less favorable reasons, be it the overly intricate hairstyle that might be perceived as too casual for a boardroom; a palette of makeup more befitting of a fashion runway than a corporate setting; the jewelry that clinks and clatters distractingly during presentations; a bold fashion statement that might overshadow the substance of a meeting; a blouse buttoned improperly than can seem careless; a skirt that's just a bit too short that may risk professionalism for fashion; nail art that's more a spectacle than a subtle accent; a cloud of overpowering perfume; or even a laptop covered in an array of personal stickers, which could undermine the polished leadership image one aims to project in a client meeting—all these details, however small, could overshadow expertise and intent and inadvertently shift the focus away from a woman's professional contributions.

It's these memorable yet incongruent details that could lead someone like Peter to recall an individual not for their professional acumen but for their sartorial choices, thinking, "Ah, yes, that's the person with the strikingly vivid hair color."

Such details, however small and even irrelevant, have the potential to cast a long shadow, sometimes causing the positive aspects of an interaction to fade from memory.

Is this fair? Certainly not. However, humans are built to think this way—this includes you, and it includes me.

Let's go back to another experience in a medical practice. Decades ago, I found myself in need of a physical therapist to treat my knee pain. Back then, when the internet was still a distant dream, I recall the quaint process of selecting a practitioner based solely on insurance coverage and the luck of the draw in a paper telephone directory.

At my appointment, I stumbled into a place that felt more like someone's home than a clinic. I navigated through a cluttered living room adorned with an eclectic assortment of plants, art, and odd collections—a creative chaos, to say the least.

Finally, I arrived at the treatment room, painted in sterile mint green, housing one of those physical therapy treatment tables enveloped in disposable paper.

Right there on this paper, which I thought was there for hygienic reasons, my eyes swiftly caught an unexpected sight: the remnants of a chicken bone. You read that right: the remains of what once was supposedly a chicken wing. Despite my initial shock—and I wish I could say I left instantly—I found myself discreetly disposing of the evidence in the therapist's trash can.

Moments later, the therapist entered with a friendly greeting, apologizing briefly for his absence due to a quick lunch break he took between patients.

I don't remember much about the treatment itself. To be fair, it might have been wonderful, his medical analysis might have been on point, and his treatment plan might have made sense. But did I ever return? The answer is no.

Or take the case of my former dentist, who undoubtedly excelled in his dental work. However, every time I reclined in his treatment chair, my attention was drawn to his complexion. It was clear he struggled with severe acne. Now, acne isn't a conscious choice one makes. It's a medical condition influenced by a variety of factors, as you know. Yet despite this understanding, I couldn't help but wonder why my dentist hadn't sought out treatments to alleviate his condition.

Every visit to his office left me grappling with conflicting thoughts. On the one hand, I admired his skill and expertise in dentistry. On the other hand, I couldn't shake the feeling of discomfort caused by the visible signs of his untreated acne. It wasn't that I judged him for his condition; rather, I questioned why someone in his position hadn't taken steps to address it.

Or consider my first-ever therapist, whom I sought out during the pandemic. Our initial consultations, spanning the first half year, unfolded virtually, with screens serving as our meeting ground. Our conversations provided much-needed support during those trying times.

When the opportunity arose to finally meet in person as the world slowly reopened, we both were eager to see each other face to face. It was during that first in-person meeting I couldn't help but notice she was a flagrant nail-biter. Although she didn't engage in the habit in my presence, the telltale signs of its effects were evident. It may seem like a minor detail, one easily overlooked amidst the patience, calmness, and guidance she had provided me with over the screen, but from that moment on, I found myself unable to shake the thought: how could someone visibly grappling with such stress and discomfort, evident in the damage inflicted upon her nails, effectively assist me in overcoming the mental challenges I faced?

Now, I'm no medical expert, and I understand there could be various reasons behind her condition. Nonetheless, the visible manifestation of her struggles left me questioning the foundation of our therapeutic relationship. As time passed, I found myself hesitating to return for further sessions, ultimately choosing not to do so without ever articulating the reason why to her.

Have you ever walked into a boardroom only to be subtly irritated by the sight of someone's overly casual hair style, a small rebellion against the corporate uniform that left you questioning their performance? Or perhaps you've sat down in a colleague's office, noticing the leftover coffee cups—each stained mug a silent testament to countless meetings and deadlines — or perhaps, a sign of a chaotic rhythm of work that made you wonder about their capacity to handle one more task or deadline.

Can you recall a time at a fancy restaurant where the waiter's stained tie painted a picture at odds with the establishment's refined aura. Think back to the trainer at a seminar whose brilliant insights were momentarily overshadowed by the typos in their slide deck. Or the real estate agent who showcased pristine homes while their car, cluttered with personal belongings, narrated a separate story of chaos amidst order. These seemingly insignificant visual cues can speak volumes, often louder than words.

Each wrinkle, stain, or out-of-place element becomes a character in the story we tell ourselves about the individuals we encounter, sometimes becoming a defining chapter that overshadows their skills and reputation.

Successful women in leadership understand and accept that everything is rooted in the details. Those little details can make us stand out for reasons both right and wrong. The challenge is that those details will be of different importance from person to person.

Take, once again, the instances of the chicken bone, the acne, and the nail biting, which may not raise an eyebrow for some patients, but for me, they were enough to influence my perception.

Yet, in contrast, I find myself in the care of a different therapist now. Despite her office being a vibrant collection of eclectic items and her appearance diverging from any conventional expectations, she has a remarkable ability to instantly create an atmosphere of safety, warmth, and comfort. With her, none of those details seem to hold any weight. Every visit leaves me feeling supported, understood, and at ease.

One jarring detail can be enough to get you consigned to the category of loser—or create an unwanted distraction. Within the realm of patient care, it's the myriad of small details that can make a monumental difference in the overall experience. Although some of these details may seem trivial at first glance, they possess the power to exert a significant influence on patients' perceptions and satisfaction levels.

Yet despite the challenge of meticulously considering each of these minor aspects, doing so presents a remarkable opportunity for you. In the workplace, where many professionals, regardless of their gender identity, are deemed average, it's these subtle nuances that allow you to stand out—for all the right reasons.

The ABCDEs of Your Professional Identity

As we piece together the many small interactions we have, a clear picture begins to form. This picture is your professional identity. Think of it as a puzzle in which each piece, no matter how small, has its own place and reason. Each detail works together to show who you are as a woman in leadership. And each element does not exist in isolation; rather, they interlock to form the complete picture that others perceive. Your professional imprint encompasses a multifaceted blend of choices you make—small or large—that shape how you're perceived and valued in your role. And this professional identity is the sum total of your choices in the following five areas:

- appearance;
- behavior;
- communication;
- digital footprint; and
- environment.

Here's an easy way to remember these five key elements: just think "ABCDE."

APPEARANCE: Your appearance is your first opportunity to make a statement without saying a word. It's the canvas upon which your personality is painted and the initial impression you leave on others. From the moment someone lays eyes on you, they're subconsciously processing a wealth of information about who you are and what you represent. Let's start with your body image—the first thing people notice about you. Whether you're tall or short, slim or sturdy, these physical attributes shape the initial perception others form. But it's not just about the shape or size of your body; your overall health, both physical and mental, also radiates through your appearance. A vibrant glow of vitality or a worn-down facade can speak volumes about your well-being.

Clothing is your armor in the battlefield of first impressions. The fit, brand, style, quality, patterns, and colors of your clothes silently communicate your taste, personality, and attention to detail. Accessories are the finishing touches that add flair to your ensemble. Whether it's a statement necklace, a sleek watch, or a pair of polished shoes, these embellishments speak volumes about your personality and style. Maintaining your wardrobe is an often-overlooked aspect of personal presentation. Well-kept garments demonstrate your commitment to professionalism and, again, attention to detail. Your personal grooming is the final touch that completes your appearance. Skin care, makeup, dental hygiene, hair care, and nail maintenance all contribute to your overall presentation. Your appearance is a silent language that speaks volumes about who you are and how you approach life—and your career. It allows you to set the stage for meaningful connections and interactions.

BEHAVIOR: At the core of your behavior lies your attitude—the vibrant colors that illuminate your outlook on life, ranging from sunny optimism to somber clouds of negativity. Your attitude not only sets the tone for your interactions but also serves as a compass guiding you through life's and your career's twists and turns. Adding depth to your behavior is your charisma (or lack thereof), drawing others into your orbit with your irresistible charm. Navigating this rich tapestry of behavior requires emotional intelligence—the wisdom to read between the lines and steer gracefully through the intricate labyrinth of human interaction. But no masterpiece is complete without a sturdy foundation of ethics and morals, the bedrock upon which your character stands firm. And as you navigate the vast canvas of human interaction, diplomacy and courtesy are hopefully your guiding stars. With your behavior, you not only enhance your effectiveness as a leader but also weave a landscape of lasting relationships and meaningful connections.

COMMUNICATION: At the heart of communication lies active listening—the art of truly tuning in to others. Through active listening, you not only hear the words spoken but also understand the emotions and intentions behind them. Adding depth to your communication are your body language and facial expressions, the nonverbal and silent-yet-eloquent language of gestures, postures, and movements. Your body and face speak volumes, conveying emotions and attitudes that words alone cannot capture. And what melody is complete without your voice—the instrument you play every single day? Your voice, with its range of tones, pitches, and cadences. From the gentle lilt of encouragement to the commanding resonance of authority, each vocal element adds depth and richness to your message. Words themselves are the very essence of communication, and your language palette is the paintbrush with which you craft your message. Yet it's not just what you say but how you say it that shapes the narrative of your communication. Your communication habits, whether empathetic and concise or passive and manipulative, set the tone for your interactions, guiding the flow of every conversation and shaping the dynamics of relationships. Your accent or dialect may add richness and diversity to these conversations. Finally, your written communication is the ink that flows through the veins of our interconnected world. By intentionally weaving together these elements of communication, you create a masterpiece of connection and under-standing.

DIGITAL FOOTPRINT: Your digital footprint is like a breadcrumb trail scattered across the internet, with each crumb leaving its mark on your online reputation. From intentional actions to those unwittingly left behind, each interaction shapes not only your digital online persona in the first step, but also your offline persona as a consequence. At the heart of this trail lies email communication, a digital handshake that speaks volumes about your professionalism and reliability. Similarly, your mobile communication offers glimpses into your accessibility and efficiency.

Venturing into the realm of social media, with your posts, comments, likes, and shares, can enhance your online reputation, positioning you as a credible and insightful voice within your digital community. In the realm of virtual meetings, your digital footprint takes on a new dimension, showcasing your adaptability and professionalism in remote settings. Meanwhile, chats and forums serve as arenas for digital discourse, where your contributions reflect your expertise, engagement, credibility, and influence within online communities. Ultimately, the frequency, savviness, and authenticity of your digital interactions shape your unintentional footprint, influencing how you're perceived in the digital realm. By actively managing and curating your digital presence, you can craft a compelling online persona that aligns with your professional aspirations and values, leaving a lasting impression on those who encounter your digital trail.

ENVIRONMENT: Your environment isn't just where you are—it's the vibrant backdrop against which your professional journey unfolds, filled with both tangible and intangible elements that shape your daily experiences and leave an indelible mark. Your network, for example, isn't just a list of contacts; it's a living ecosystem that provides support, fosters collaboration, and unlocks doors of opportunity at every turn. Then there's the spaces you inhabit—the places where you live, work, and everything in between. They're more than just physical locations; they're sanctuaries of productivity, creativity, and inspiration. And let's not forget about the journey itself—the daily commute, the occasional getaway, and the leisure pursuits that recharge your batteries. From the thrill of exploration to the tranquility of downtime, these experiences add color to the canvas of your professional life, infusing it with excitement, balance, and rejuvenation. Your environment isn't just a backdrop; it's a character in the story of your professional journey, shaping the plot and influencing the outcome at every twist and turn. So take a moment to look around. What do you see? How does it make you feel?

And most importantly, how can you optimize it to support your goals, reflect your values, and lead you toward success and fulfillment?

Internal and External Consistency

Consistency is the backbone of any credible professional imprint. The key is to ensure your appearance, behavior, communication, digital footprint, and environment all sing the same tune. You can't present yourself as reliable and trustworthy in your clothing, but then behave unpredictably or unprofessionally during interactions. You can't curate an online persona that conflicts with who you are in the real world. Surrounding yourself with luxury and glamour while aspiring to a reputation of humility and service sends mixed messages. Only when all elements of your professional identity align harmoniously does the message of who you are and what you stand for become unmistakable, compelling, and memorable.

This consistency also extends beyond your personal presentation to maintaining a coherent professional identity both within your organization and in the wider world.

Your internal professional identity pertains to how you present yourself, behave, and communicate within the intricate ecosystem of your organization. This includes interactions within your office and your team, collaborative projects with cross-departmental teams, and consultations with colleagues or top management. People in the workplace look up to leaders who demonstrate consistency.

Your external professional identity, in contrast, pertains to how you represent yourself and your organization to external stakeholders. Each public interaction, be it a conference presentation or a community event, shapes how others perceive you, the organization you're part of, and it's entire leadership.

Consistency in your appearance, behavior, communication, digital presence, and environment, both internally and externally, reinforces trust and credibility, enhancing both your personal reputation and that of the organization.

This principle may seem straightforward and achievable to you, yet one of the most significant challenges leaders face is ensuring consistency not only in their own choices but also across their team members. When the entire team adheres to agreed-upon standards, it fosters unity and professionalism, enhancing the team dynamic and how others perceive the organization. Conversely, when team members deviate from these norms, it can lead to confusion and undermine team cohesion, the organization's image—and yes, your professional identity.

It's essential for your team members to understand that their appearance, behavior, communication, digital presence, and environment inside and outside of their respective organizations reflect on the organizations they represent. And although many team members may diligently adhere to internal protocols and standards within the workplace, there can be a tendency for some to inadvertently overlook these standards outside of professional settings. So, it's vital for your team members to recognize that their choices in public settings directly reflect upon the reputation and credibility of the organizations they represent—and hence on you as a leader.

At any given time, your team members may encounter clients, stakeholders, or community members outside the professional setting. It's crucial that they also maintain professionalism and discretion in these interactions—anytime, anywhere, and with anyone, upholding the reputation of the organization they are affiliated with. This includes your team members' activities on social media platforms, which also have a significant impact on internal and external perceptions of their respective organizations. Even when posting in a personal capacity, they should be mindful of how their online behavior can be interpreted as a reflection on themselves and their organization.

Maintaining internal and external consistency is not solely the responsibility of leaders; it extends to every team member. If this resonates with you as a familiar challenge, another chapter of this book will delve deeper into strategies and techniques for effectively addressing these challenges with your team, providing tips and insights to support you in having these sensitive conversations. The aim is to ensure you continue to foster a culture of consistency and excellence among all sectors where women can be leaders, encompassing corporate, government, education, nonprofit, and entrepreneurial endeavors—uniting both your team and yourself.

Chapter 3
Leaders Look Confident

Confidence Isn't Thinking You Are Better. It's Realizing You Have No Reason to Compare Yourself.

Chapter 3: Leaders Look Confident

What is confidence, what does it mean to look confident, and why would it matter for a leader? It's indeed a complex question. Confidence, in the broadest sense, is not merely about possessing a firm belief in one's abilities or the decisions one makes. It transcends the boundaries of self-assurance to encompass an aura of competence and unwavering authority that inspires trust, respect, and a sense of security among all stakeholders—be it colleagues, team members, managers, clients, or the wider community. In the high-stakes professional world, where decisions often carry the weight of life-altering consequences, the confidence of a leader becomes, in fact, a cornerstone.

Research has explored various aspects of women and confidence, particularly in the professional arena. You might certainly see yourself as an outlier to common stereotypes, and indeed, many women are. However, an aggregation of research suggests that, broadly speaking, confidence is not the strongest trait among women, particularly in comparison to their male counterparts. This is not to say that individual women cannot possess a strong sense of self-confidence, but studies, such as those conducted by the National Bureau of Economic Research, have revealed that women tend, for example, to underrate their performance. Women consistently rated their performance on a test lower than men did, even when both groups had the same average scores. Men rated themselves, on average, 61 out of 100, whereas women gave themselves a rating of 46 out of 100.

Harvard Business School assistant professor Katherine B. Coffman found that women might steer clear of certain professions due to a lack of confidence in their abilities, especially in fields such as science, math, and technology, where men are stereotypically believed to perform better. This self-doubt can also make women more hesitant to share their ideas in group discussions or to accept and believe in positive feedback about their abilities, even when they are high achievers in these subjects.

These are just a few results that encapsulate a spectrum of influences shaping participants' confidence—after all, confidence is a multifaceted construct. Confidence is a complex construct, built from a mosaic of internal and external factors. Yet, as we turn the pages of this book to focus on the "look of leadership," let's delve into how visual appearance, a pivotal yet complex element, plays a role in this narrative.

Your appearance is just one of the elements that contribute to confidence, yet it plays a significant role. The "look of confidence" may at first glance seem superficial to some. However, its impact is far-reaching, deeply rooted in the psychological interplay between self-perception and public perception. The notion to "just dress confidently and yourself and others will instantly recognize your confidence" oversimplifies the depth of how confidence is conveyed and perceived. Nonetheless, the visual aspect of leadership acts as a powerful filter through which both the leader and those they lead interpret your confidence (or lack thereof).

Let's first explore the internal dimension of dressing with confidence. It's a universally acknowledged truth that when we look good, we feel good. This isn't a shallow vanity but a reflection of how closely intertwined our self-esteem and self-perception are with our external appearance. Clothes do more than just cover us up; they can make us feel good or uneasy, especially at work. Researcher Kim K. P. Johnson and her team, responsible for the article "Dress, Body and Self: Research on the Social Psychology of Dress," found that when professionals dressed right for their job, they felt more sure of themselves.

They associated psychological discomfort with wearing inappropriate dress for work. Mary Katherine Brock's research confirms that young teenage girls' confidence is heavily influenced by the clothes they wear. Even color seems to matter, as Craig Roberts and his research team point out, because certain colors, such as red, could boost confidence in individuals.

You might remember the research I mentioned earlier by Hajo Adam and Adam D. Galinsky, who introduced the concept of enclothed cognition, which means what we wear can change the way we think and feel. Let's take a closer look at how they performed this study. Their research focused on the significance of wearing white coats in the medical arena. Their study delves into how this attire impacts mental processes. They discovered that wearing a white coat can sharpen a person's focus and carefulness. However, the effect varied based on the described purpose of the coat: white coats labeled as belonging to doctors enhanced attentiveness more than those described as painters' coats. This indicates that the influence of clothing on cognitive function hinges on both the symbolic association and the physical act of wearing the garment.

In the realm of leadership, where the environment may be as challenging as it is unpredictable, the armor of a well-considered wardrobe serves not just as a physical outfit but also as a psychological bolster. What we decide to put on every day can shape how we feel about ourselves and how we interact with others. It's not just about looking good; it's about feeling good too.

For women in leadership across all sectors, from the tailored dress of an executive woman to the business casual outfit of a nonprofit manager, this might mean clothing that conveys professionalism, competence, and authority that also enhances one's self-assurance and confidence.

On the flip side, the external dimension of dressing with confidence concerns how you are perceived by others—clients, team members, managers, colleagues, and the broader community.

In any almost any sector, trust, credibility, and authority are the hallmarks of effective leadership, and appearance can significantly influence these perceptions. The interplay between self-perception and external perception creates a symbiotic relationship in which internal confidence and the way others view us reinforce each other. This cycle of positive reinforcement between embodying the persona of a leader and being recognized as one accentuates the extension of confidence through one's appearance.

Leaders Are Confident about Their Body

Let's start our discussion about confidence by ignoring all the things you can buy at a department store or online and focus on the suit you were born with: your body.

A woman who is comfortable in her own skin commands a presence that is both authoritative and reassuring—and, after all, confident. This presence is critical in professional settings, where the confidence conveyed can significantly influence perceptions, dynamics, and even outcomes. In addition, by embodying confidence in their physical selves, women leaders can set a powerful example for colleagues, team members, and the community.

Recognizing the body as a fundamental aspect of your identity and a vessel through which you offer leadership is the first step toward deeper self-confidence. You need to acknowledge your unique body characteristics—your strengths and your limitations—and embrace them as integral parts of who you are.

Because truth be told, although there certainly are some tricks when it comes to dressing your body, you'll never be able to fully change the fundamentals: someone short will never be tall; someone overweight will never look skinny. This acceptance is not resignation but a celebration of diversity and your individuality—and your focus should be on your body's health more than on a measurement tape.

However, research does provide insightful correlations between height, weight, and leadership perception. Sylvia Ann Hewlett and her team surveyed college-educated professionals and senior executives about executive presence. They found that women are judged more critically by their weight, whereas men are more likely to be judged by their height. Of those surveyed, 16 percent said it's important for men to be tall, compared to just 6 percent for women.

Height is often perceived as a silent herald of leadership. It's associated with authority, confidence, and dominance. But the intrinsic value of leadership is not measured in inches. Even though height may be a factor, enduring leadership is built on the foundation of competence, empathy, and integrity. These are qualities that transcend physical dimensions.

And the reality is that height is a fixed attribute, with limited scope for change. Visual strategies such as posture, wardrobe choices, and the strategic use of footwear can subtly influence the perception of height. But remember, opting for heels that hamper your natural walk can do more harm than good to your leadership image. It's about striking a balance—wear what elevates your confidence without compromising your comfort or poise.

In contrast, weight, which might be perceived as a reflection of personal discipline and lifestyle, often becomes a topic of discussion in relation to credibility and authority. In various professional spheres, particularly those with a focus on health, fitness, or overall well-being, weight can carry connotations of personal discipline and lifestyle, influencing perceptions of credibility and authority.

For instance, consider industries such as personal training, health care, or nutrition, where professionals often serve as role models for healthful living; in these fields, the expectation might be that personal appearance aligns with professional advice. Similarly, executive roles that demand a high degree of discipline and self-control might also scrutinize physical fitness as a proxy for these traits.

In such industries, the unspoken norms suggest that maintaining a certain physique may be intertwined with professional effectiveness in the minds of others.

In the public opinion, unlike height, weight is seen as a variable and is frequently more directly linked to perceptions of health. Here, leaders have a dual role: to model a commitment to well-being and to challenge the stereotypes that unjustly conflate physical appearance with professional competence.

Bias related to weight manifests in two opposing but equally damaging stereotypes: those who are heavier may be perceived as lacking self-control or health awareness, whereas those who are thinner may face misjudgments of being too delicate to manage the stress and responsibilities of leadership positions. Both of these stereotypes are unjust and overlook the individual's actual capabilities and contributions.

The research of Patricia V. Roehling and her team highlights how obesity affects perceptions of promotability, demonstrating that obese candidates are often seen as less suitable for promotions compared to individuals with other physical conditions. This bias also extends to leadership perceptions, where obese individuals are significantly underrepresented in top positions within Fortune 100 companies. Additionally, studies by T. L. Brink, further supported by Eden B. King, reveal that obesity can heavily influence views of one's leadership abilities.

Despite the impact of weight on professional perceptions as highlighted by various studies, the most crucial factor is your own relationship with your body weight because it significantly influences your self-confidence.

This internal perception of self-worth and assurance can override external biases and shape how you're viewed in leadership and professional capacities. Hence, for those seeking to align their weight with their health goals and professional identity, the options include the following:

Carry your weight with poise and confidence, no matter the number on the scale. Keep in mind, however, that the right fit of clothing can significantly affect how your weight is perceived by yourself and others. Ill-fitting clothes can add pounds or create an unflattering silhouette that distracts and often backfires. Conversely, well-tailored clothes can enhance your presence, contributing positively to your confidence and overall perception. The key is a strategic selection of clothing that fits impeccably, thus avoiding adding unnecessary bulk or implying a lack of attention to detail—both of which can detract from your professional identity.

And ignore any outdated and oversimplified methods of categorizing body shapes. You are more than an "apple" or a "pear"—you are a woman, a leader, a force, and an individual whose worth is defined by accomplishments and abilities, not by the contours of a silhouette. Your shape does not confine your potential; it is your presence, your expertise, and your actions that carve out the real shape of your influence and impact.

This advice, although once popular, not only pigeonholes you but also often overlooks the nuances and individuality of each person's personal style. It disregards the fact that whereas some women may wish to downplay their "pear" shape, others may want to embrace and accentuate it with pride. No one-size-fits-all concept can dictate whether you should highlight or downplay your shape. Your body, your rules—your style should be a reflection of you, not a fruit comparison chart.

Opt to lose or gain weight, yet the focus should be on health rather than solely on aesthetics. Positive changes in weight can lead to a boost in self-esteem and an improvement in how leaders are perceived by others. And as you know firsthand, this process should be undertaken with mindfulness and health as the priority, ensuring the journey toward weight change is sustainable and reflects a genuine commitment to your personal well-being.

When considering a weight change, it's essential to approach this subject holistically. It's not just about the number on the scale but about nurturing a lifestyle that promotes overall well-being.

Weight management can be empowering and affirming, especially when done through methods that prioritize nourishment, energy levels, and inner balance. It's about finding what feels good and sustainable for your body and lifestyle. A well-nourished body supports a sharp mind, essential for decision-making and endurance through long days.

Moreover, exercise and a balanced diet are known to improve mood and reduce stress, contributing positively to one's executive presence. Finally, it's about inclusivity in health and wellness, recognizing that healthy bodies come in all sizes and that the objective isn't a specific aesthetic, but rather a state of health where you feel most vibrant and capable. This approach not only ensures that the journey toward any weight change is sustainable but also reinforces the idea that leadership is embodied in a myriad of forms.

In the end, the measure of a leader is not taken from physical attributes such as weight or height but from the impact one makes—the individuals you mentor, the teams you empower, and the contributions you make to your field. Observable physical characteristics are superficial metrics that do not reflect the depth and breadth of your influence and capabilities. The essence of your leadership radiates from a core of integrity, the expanse of expertise, and the elevation of your goals and visions.

However, if your outward appearance can amplify your inherent confidence, it's a resource worth harnessing. Visual illusions can be powerful tools for enhancing this confidence. They're the subtle yet strategic choices we make in our wardrobe that influence self-confidence and outer perception. Embracing these visual techniques does not undermine your authenticity; rather, it underscores your self-awareness and the deliberate cultivation of your professional identity.

It's not about misrepresentation but about presenting yourself in a manner that reflects your best qualities and intentions. After all, leadership is a performance art, and every leader is both the sculptor and the sculpture of their professional identity.

Leaders Are Confident about Their Age

Age can be another influential factor in shaping perceptions, often correlated with experience and wisdom on one end and energy and innovation on the other. It bears a psychological weight, influencing both the self-perception of women and the expectations of those they work with and serve.

The spectrum of age in the professional world is broad and diverse. On one end, there is the seasoned woman in leadership, whose years are viewed as a compendium of expertise, a living library of knowledge and experience garnered through years of dedication and hands-on work. Their age is often associated with a profound understanding and a reassuring presence that commands respect in any professional challenge.

On the flip side, youth in the professional arena is lauded for its connection with agility, both mentally and physically. Younger women are often seen as the vanguard of innovation, bringing fresh perspectives from recent education and a zeal for progressive methodologies. Their age represents a drive for momentum and an ambition to innovate and expand the horizons of their respective fields. Yet these perceived roles are not without their complications.

This dichotomy can create an internal struggle for women as they advance in their careers. Seasoned leaders may feel compelled to demonstrate ongoing relevance in rapidly changing industries, whereas emerging leaders often work to assert their authority and gain trust within hierarchies that have historically valued longevity.

Each stage of a leader's journey is accompanied by its own set of perceptions and expectations, both self-imposed and from external sources. It's within this intricate landscape that leaders must establish their presence, capitalizing on the strengths that come with their experience level while challenging any perceived constraints associated with their age.

Age, much like height and unlike weight, is an immutable number, a marker of time that, contrary to popular belief, has no direct correlation with success. Across the spectrum of history and into the modern day, leaders have emerged at various stages of their lives, showcasing that age is not a determinant of capability. Success in leadership is age agnostic; instead, it is reliant on the unique value and experience each individual brings to their role.

The key to navigating age is once again embracing it—owning one's years with confidence. This means drawing focus on the richness of your experience, the depth of your knowledge, and the unique value you add to your team and your organization; it means celebrating milestones and using your accumulated wisdom to influence and inspire.

It's human nature to wish to be perceived as younger or older, but a challenge arises when efforts to alter your age's perception lead to inauthenticity. Yes, visual elements can be used to suggest a more youthful or mature image, but these should be approached with moderation. Excessive attempts, such as dressing overly younger or older, extreme dieting or fitness regimens that are unsustainable, the use of heavy makeup to conceal natural features, the adoption of fashion trends that do not align with one's personal style or age, or overindulgence in plastic surgery, can convey a lack of confidence in one's natural progression through life—a message particularly conflicting in leadership, where authenticity and trust are paramount. These efforts, despite aiming to enhance one's appearance, may instead project a sense of insecurity. When women in leadership resort to extreme measures to alter their age appearance, it can overshadow their actual competencies and achievements.

It's a delicate balance between using visual elements to slightly improve your self-confidence and adjust your age's perception and overstepping into the territory where those elements detract from your authenticity.

For young women who are new to the workplace, lean into the fresh perspective and innovative ideas that often accompany youth. You can build credibility by demonstrating eagerness to learn, bringing energy to your work, and showcasing your up-to-date knowledge and skills. As a seasoned professional woman, your years of experience are a testament to your resilience and wisdom. It's important to celebrate and leverage this depth of knowledge, network, and leadership skills you have cultivated over time. Emphasize these attributes because they're invaluable and often sought-after qualities in leadership.

View your age as an asset, not a barrier. Aim to present yourself in a way that highlights the intrinsic value you bring to your role. Resist succumbing to societal pressures about age. In embracing your years with dignity and self-respect, you also set a positive example for your colleagues, team members, and clients that it's not the number of years in your life that defines your value, but rather the quality and impact of one's performance that truly counts.

Leaders Are Confident about Their Gender

It will come as no surprise to you that gender dynamics play a significant role in leadership perception. Traditionally, nurturing roles were often seen as women's domains, whereas positions demanding authority were typically reserved for men. In the modern professional landscape, these outdated stereotypes are being actively contested and redefined. Despite the progress, subtler shades of these stereotypes linger, manifesting in nuanced biases and expectations that persist beneath the surface of our evolving workplace culture. It's an ongoing process to root out these remnants and move toward a truly equitable professional environment.

In research conducted by Janice Fanning Madden at the University of Pennsylvania, an insightful spotlight was shone on the sales teams within large brokerage firms. In these environments, where income is intrinsically tied to performance and commission, an imbalance was uncovered. Women, despite demonstrating equal aptitude in achieving results, were frequently handed accounts with less potential compared to their male counterparts.

Likewise, research from Joanna Barsh and Lareina Yee by McKinsey and Company confirmed that invisible barriers are holding women back, rather than overt sexism alone.

The "Howard vs. Heidi" case study, spearheaded by Frank Flynn, an associate professor at Columbia Business School, delves into the intricate dance between competence and likeability that women leaders often navigate. Participants in the study assessed the profile of a candidate—described identically in all respects but name—first as Howard, then as Heidi.

Howard emerged from this scrutiny not only as competent and effective but also as someone subjects found likeable and were eager to collaborate with. Conversely, Heidi, despite being recognized for her competence and effectiveness, was not met with the same warmth or enthusiasm for future partnership. This singular shift in gender naming laid bare an underlying bias: high-achieving women are often subjected to a stricter social ledger, where their success could diminish their likeability, a dilemma less frequently faced by their male counterparts.

A Deloitte survey indicated that women in hybrid work environments face more microaggressions than their counterparts who work solely on-site or remotely. Although hybrid work has become common for all of us, the findings highlight that it further contributes to feelings of isolation and exclusion among women.

Although significant barriers to gender equity have been dismantled over the years, often under public scrutiny leading to tangible consequences for organizations, it's the subtler, less visible forms of inequality that persistently erode the foundations of equity.

These can be harder to detect and even more challenging to address because they often go unnoticed in the public eye and are deeply embedded in workplace cultures and attitudes. Hence, women still must consistently navigate these gender-based perceptions, ensuring that the quality of their work and professionalism are the primary criteria for evaluation, not their gender.

As a woman in leadership, you may encounter the double-bind paradox too, where you're expected to be nurturing yet decisive, authoritative yet compassionate. The key to overcoming this is by embracing your gender identity with confidence and showcasing your unique leadership style—despite your gender identity. This approach means not feeling pressured to conform to traditionally masculine modes of leadership. By cultivating a personal leadership style that encompasses both empathy and assertiveness, you can redefine what it means to lead with influence and integrity—beyond your gender

Although gender bias is often discussed with a focus on women, it's crucial to recognize that men are also subjected to rigid societal expectations. Often when we discuss gender bias, we talk about women; when we think of race, we think of people of color. Often the other groups go unexamined and unanalyzed. Defined by a narrow interpretation of masculinity, for example, men are also sometimes pressured to be decisive, tough, and unyielding, leaving little space for vulnerability or emotional openness. These standards, instilled from a young age through family, education, and media, can be restrictive and damaging as well. It's important to consider the full spectrum of gender dynamics, understanding that true equality challenges constraints for all genders.

This includes nonbinary and transgender leaders who often must navigate a world that is still learning to understand and accept gender beyond the binary. Their visibility in leadership roles is itself an act of courage and representation.

For nonbinary and transgender leaders, the challenge is often about being seen and respected for their professional capabilities first, without their gender identity overshadowing their skills and contributions. By focusing on professional acumen and advocating for an environment in which all are evaluated on their contributions, we all can help ensure leadership is an area defined by the quality of care provided, not by the gender identity of those providing it. Each of us has a role in spearheading the shift toward policies and norms that honor gender diversity, embodying empathetic and inclusive leadership. Alongside these efforts, it's vital to cultivate an awareness of how gender bias still quietly casts its net through often unspoken microaggressions, shaping our interactions and workplace culture in subtle yet profound ways.

Embracing your own gender identity as part of your leadership is a profound statement of self-confidence and acceptance that sets a powerful example for others. The key lies in being comfortable in your own skin and using your unique experiences to inform and enhance your leadership approach—beyond your gender. At the core of your professional reputation should always be an unwavering commitment to excellence and the quality of leadership you express. In such an environment, gender can become one of many aspects of a leader's identity, not a hurdle to overcome but a facet that contributes to a leader's distinct perspective.

For your look of leadership, this means nurturing an authentic self-image that resonates with your values and convictions. It's about harmonizing your external presence with your inner identity, ensuring that your personal brand reflects both your competence and your authenticity. There's no need to conform to expectations of dressing more masculine or overtly feminine.

Let your gender identity enhance, not define, your leadership style. This approach not only affirms your self-worth but also inspires others to embrace their own diversity. Stand firm in your commitment to excellence, and let the uniqueness of your leadership shine, creating a path where gender diversity is celebrated as a source of strength and insight.

Leaders Are Confident about Their Style

Style is not simply about the clothes you wear or the fashion trends you follow; it's a broader expression of your identity. A leader's visual style is an authentic representation of who they are, offering a glimpse into their personality without uttering a single word.

Although it's essential to respect the professional environment and the people within it, there's ample room to weave in distinctive elements that set you apart. The primary concern is striking a balance: your wardrobe style should never overshadow your competencies but rather complement and enhance your professional narrative.

It's the distinctive elegance of a custom-tailored blazer, the strategic selection of an accessory, or the timeless charm of a statement piece of jewelry. It's in the carefully chosen brooch that commemorates a personal triumph, the glimpse of an unexpected pattern on a skirt, or the addition of a brightly colored scarf that brings life to a traditional outfit. It's the distinctive design of one's glasses or the deliberate choice of vibrant footwear that signals a meticulous eye for detail. These elements should not scream for attention but should invite intrigue and respect.

Leaders who master their style understand that going overboard can be counterproductive. It's not about pushing boundaries to the extreme but about pushing them just enough to be intriguing, memorable, and, above all, true to oneself. Your style should not distract; it should fascinate. It should not raise questions; it should assert confidence.

Defining one's personal style is a journey that many find challenging. Unlike pursuing a specific role or niche in your career, which may be influenced by passion, skill, or opportunity, style is more abstract and deeply personal, lacking a definitive guide. It's an introspective process to determine how you want to present yourself and be perceived by the world around you.

The question "What's your style?" can often leave women pondering in silence.

Style isn't about chasing the ephemeral whims of fashion nor is it defined by the price tag or the prestige of luxury brands. It's not about molding yourself to fit the silhouette of the moment or echoing the masses. Style doesn't insist on perfection; it's not a static, one-size-fits-all formula. It's not about dressing to impress others or a costume you put on for approval.

True style transcends seasonal trends and societal expectations, it's an individual expression that doesn't wane with time or shift with tides of public opinion. Style is not just about preference in color or fit; it's also about the message you want to send. And this message is rooted in the values you want to project—confidence, approachability, innovation, tradition, creativity, or care—and how these are encapsulated in your appearance.

Does your style amplify your voice? Does it echo your strategic thinking? How does your style bridge or speak to diverse backgrounds? Can your style be a tool for nonverbal communication, conveying openness to different perspectives? Your style composes a story of who you are and what you stand for, without uttering a single word.

Only by answering this underlying question can you begin to craft a style narrative that is not only unique but also aligns with your authentic self, which can lead to curating a style and professional brand that consistently and coherently communicate who you are at your core.

Chapter 4
Leaders Look Authentic

The Art of Standing Out
While Fitting In,
Without Disappearing.

Chapter 4: Leaders Look Authentic

In terms of defining your authentic "look of leadership," one of the basic notions you can take is to say, "What you see is what you get!" There's nothing worse than someone trying to be something they're not. The harder they try, the more inauthentic and phony they appear. But what does "authentic" truly mean? Authenticity is a term that has garnered much attention and various interpretations, particularly in the context of professional development and leadership. At its core, being authentic means being true to one's own personality, spirit, or character. Yet it's a concept that's far more nuanced than simply "being oneself."

Let me share two uncomfortable truths with you. The first is about the essence of authenticity. It's often touted that being authentic means you don't have to care about conforming to expectations or norms. And this notion can be very misleading.

Many hold the belief that being authentic means you can do, say, or wear whatever you want. This is a dangerous misconception, especially prevalent in the advice of "You do you!"—advice that, admittedly, I have given and received as well.

However, this mentality can lead to a disregard for the professional and social norms that facilitate effective interaction within society. Fully embracing the mantra of "You do you" might mistakenly empower an attitude of carelessness, implying that one doesn't need to take into account the broader context or the expectations of others—because "you don't have to care about anyone or anything, anywhere, at any time."

True authenticity isn't about disregarding the impact of your presence on others; it involves aligning your true self with the environment you're in, without losing the core of who you are.

Which brings us to the second notion that we each have one "authentic self," which is —sorry to break the news—a lie. The reality is that we play numerous roles in life. We're mothers, siblings, children, friends, neighbors, colleagues—and leaders. Each of these roles demands a different facet of our personality and presentation. To be truly successful, you need to adapt your "authentic self" in terms of your appearance, behavior, and communication to the context of each role. Imagine interacting with your children in the same way as with your clients, or speaking to your parents as you would to your life partner. Wearing the same outfit in the gym as you would at work. Although there may be a consistent thread of core beliefs that defines you, the expression of your authenticity will vary depending on the situation.

Authenticity, then, is not about a rigid adherence to a single, unchanging self in all contexts. The focus is on being true to your core values while also possessing the flexibility to effectively navigate different environments. In leadership, this means finding harmony between your private persona and your professional identity, ensuring that each role you play is infused with your values. This harmony allows for different versions of authenticity that are considerate of both your own self-expression and the expectations of those around you. It's not about concealing who you are; it's about respectfully acknowledging the part you play in each aspect and role of your life and doing so with sincerity and professionalism.

Like it or not, in any professional sector—as in broader society—people carry implicit expectations, scripts that are often unspoken yet heavily influence perceptions. Your appearance can either confirm or challenge these scripts. Aligning your appearance with these professional expectations isn't about diminishing your authenticity; it's about reflecting your authentic self within the framework of your role.

During my keynotes, I present participants with various images of individuals dressed in professional attire. I then pose some questions to the audience: "Which of these individuals would you entrust with your legal battles, your computer setup, or the education of your children?"

Again and again, the responses are predictably consistent, underscoring how quickly we form perceptions based on someone's appearance.

My audience's inner dialogue might go something like this: One person is dressed in a sharp-lined, charcoal-gray suit, impeccable white shirt, and red tie that exudes a strategic and commanding presence ("that's got to be the lawyer"). Right next to that person is someone in smart casual attire—a coat, a light shirt without a tie, and slacks ("clearly, that's the IT expert"). Then there's someone in a light, pastel dress that flows softly, the kind that suggests kindness and a nurturing spirit ("surely, she's the teacher").

It's these small, deliberate choices in someone's visual appearance that speak to us before a word is uttered, painting a picture of who these individuals might be in their professional worlds while expressing their authentic selves in their roles. So let's examine how you, too, can strategically align your visual presentation with your authentic selves.

Keywords Are the Keys to Authenticity

We all carry mental templates of various leaders, and although these templates might differ in detail, they share certain core attributes. Regarding the lawyer my audience envisions, her attire isn't chosen for its exceptional or creative flair; rather, it's selected for the messages it conveys: reliability, authority, trustworthiness, and consistency.

In the legal profession, the keyword that resonates is "trust," not "creativity." Contrast this with the clothes of a creative head of a buying department in a retail company.

Although still donning a suit, the fabric may be more distinctive, featuring an eclectic pattern paired with a vibrant blouse and perhaps a brightly colored standout accessory that captures the essence of "creativity"—the keyword for this role.

Leaders with a keen sense of style understand that their sartorial choices speak volumes about their professional identity. The most authentic leaders are known for either their elegant aesthetic or their inventive appearance; they choose a signature look that not only reflects their personality but also aligns with the keyword they represent. It's not a facade but a genuine reflection of their roles and the values they uphold. Let's now explore how you can harness the power of keywords to forge your professional identity and elevate your leadership presence by:

Unveiling your sector-specific keywords and expectations. In every industry, there exists some form of a mental "uniform"—a sartorial standard that may not be as overt and codified as those of police officers, firefighters, military personnel, or chefs, but it's implicitly understood. These are the "perceived uniforms," an unspoken dress code shaped by societal expectations and assumptions about certain professions. These perceived uniforms serve as a visual shorthand, helping to forge an immediate connection between professional identity and public perception and allowing women to express their expertise and role within this industry visually.

You might ask: So, what are the expected keywords in my industry?

The answer lies in the collective expectations of all stakeholders—clients, partners, colleagues—who interact with leaders across fields. These keywords become the essence of the perceived uniform for each industry. They reflect the attributes that associates, peers, and clients alike associate with professionalism and expertise.

In finance, the keyword "trustworthiness" may be instantly expected and can be visualized, for example, through structured suits and conservative colors.

In the arts, the keyword "creativity" might feature bold statements and eclectic pairings that showcase innovation in your appearance.

For those in environmental advocacy, "sustainability" is key, and clothing choices made from earth-conscious materials can communicate a genuine commitment to conservation.

For women in construction, clothing that balances "visionary" design and "pragmatic" utility underscores the innovative yet hands-on nature of their work.

In the dynamic world of sports management, "energetic" and "team-oriented" pieces reflect a blend of strategy and action, mirroring the vibrancy of the industry.

Attire in the space industry aligns with "futuristic" and "high-tech" themes, often incorporating sleek and modern elements that speak to the forward-thinking nature of the field.

Meanwhile, women in government roles may opt for "dignified" attire, projecting a sense of steadfast public service and leadership, with a nod to the traditional yet evolving narrative of governmental responsibility.

Each of these keywords encapsulates an industry's or role's values and the expectations of its audience. By carefully crafting a visual appearance that aligns with these keywords, you can craft a leadership image that not only meets professional standards but also resonates with the unique characteristics of your field—thereby reinforcing your role and strengthening your personal brand identity.

However, defining these expectations and keywords can be intricate, influenced by numerous factors including your specific sector, the culture of your organization, your geographical location, or the diverse backgrounds of the clientele and colleagues you engage with regularly.

Defining your distinctive edge and personal keyword. The most authentic women in leadership understand that their appearance is a powerful form of nonverbal communication. Through their chosen style, they convey a narrative about who they are, and they're clear about the keywords that describe this narrative. Each keyword tells a part of your story. Each look confirms the essence of their story. If your professional ethos is grounded in trust, respect, and loyalty, your appearance should reinforce these qualities. Alternatively, if you pride yourself on being individualistic, fearless, and imaginative, your choices might be more bold and innovative, reflecting a pioneering spirit.

Have you considered the unique traits that define you at work and how they translate into the visual messages you wish to instantly imprint? Reflecting on these defining traits that make you unique in your professional life and how these translate visually is crucial. Doing so allows you to pinpoint a style that not only makes you self-confident but also conveys the key messages you intend to communicate. It's a process critical in shaping not just any personal style but one that resonates with confidence and the professional identity you want to project.

Harmonizing your personal essence and industry's expectations. Once your industry's (or company's or profession's or specific role's) keyword and your personal keywords are established, the next phase is alignment—that is, checking whether these keywords echo and resonate with the ethos of your profession. If you are fortunate, the keywords you have selected to describe your authentic self align with the persona expected in your professional sphere. When there's a match, it can feel like a natural extension of your identity. Conversely, if there's a disconnect, it can manifest as a nagging sense of being out of place, prompting you to question why you feel like you don't quite belong.

In general, from all possible keywords emerge seven categories of perception personas, each symbolizing a specific set of values and attributes that women either find themselves in or are often expected to embody. These personas are not just about the clothes worn; they represent the overall professional identity that you are anticipated to uphold at work and in interactions. The seven personas can be categorized into two distinct types: your primary persona, which forms the core of your identity, and your secondary persona, which complements the primary one.

Your primary persona is akin to your DNA—it's the bedrock of your identity. It's reflected in the consistent strands of your character, coloring your instinctive choices and the way you inherently engage with the world.

Your secondary persona is more fluid, sculpted by the ebb and flow of your external experiences, age, education, preferences, and the continuous curve of personal growth. It grants you the flexibility to adapt, to mold your choices to fit the myriad of scenarios you encounter throughout your career and life.

Whereas your primary persona remains unaltered, steadfast in its authenticity, your secondary persona acts as a versatile complement. It doesn't overshadow your core; rather, it expands upon it, allowing you a greater spectrum of expression. Together, they form a cohesive identity that is both true to your essence and attuned to the nuances of your professional environment.

Before we embark on outlining the personas, it's important to recognize that these personas are not rigid classifications. They do more than just categorize us. They influence our perspective on the world, and, consequently, these personas are often reflected in our external presentation—the clothes we choose, the hairstyles we adopt, and the accessories we carry, all of which are outward expressions of our inner narrative.

It's also quite possible you find yourself in more than just one primary or secondary persona—more on this complexity later. For now, let's get started with the three primary personas that exist.

The Explorer: Approachable and Relaxed

Explorers embody a spirit that is both adventurous and pragmatic, often reflected in a style that prioritizes comfort and practicality. She chooses her wardrobe less for the latest fashion trends and more for the functionality and durability of the garments. Imagine her attire as ready for an impromptu trek as it is for a casual business meeting: comfortable jeans paired with a resilient T-shirt and sturdy footwear that speaks to a life in motion.

In her wardrobe, you'll find clothes, many in earthy tones, that serve a purpose: utility jackets with pockets aplenty, fabrics that can withstand the elements, and colors that blend with the natural world. Maintenance is fuss-free, with a preference for clothing that endures the wear and tear of her explorations without demanding meticulous care.

Her approach to body image is straightforward and unpretentious. Her physique, whether it's conditioned by active pursuits or carries the robustness of a life well lived, is a testament to her experiences rather than a curated image. In her world, the body is less a canvas for fashion and more a vessel for adventure, a mindset that brings a unique confidence and an unbothered attitude toward societal beauty standards.

When it comes to makeup, the Explorer favors a minimalistic approach, if any at all. A touch of tinted moisturizer for a healthy glow, a swipe of waterproof mascara, and a balm to protect her lips are all she needs to maintain her natural look, ready for whatever the day may bring.

Her accessories, like the sporty watch on her wrist to the backpack slung over her shoulder, are chosen for resilience and utility, echoing the Explorer's readiness for life's spontaneous adventures.

For hair and nails, the Explorer opts for easy maintenance, prioritizing health and manageability. A simple ponytail, braid, or short, practical haircut suits her active lifestyle. Her manicure and pedicure are neat yet unfussy, often favoring clear polish or natural tones that don't show wear easily.

- **Keyword:** comfort
- **Perceived traits:** active, adventurous, casual, approachable, optimistic, energetic, natural, direct, spontaneous, enthusiastic
- **Perceived challenges:** disorganized, dull, graceless, mannerless, ordinary, unambitious, unpolished, weak

The Traditionalist: Trustworthy and Reliable

The Traditionalist carries an air of timeless elegance, exuding a commitment to enduring styles that is immediately apparent. She isn't swayed by passing trends but is firmly rooted in classic fashion principles. Envision her in attire that pays homage to the past while fitting impeccably into the now: a well-tailored blazer that defies the ebb and flow of fads, a silk blouse that whispers sophistication, or leather pumps polished to perfection.

In her wardrobe, you will discover a carefully selected ensemble of pieces that defy the transient whims of fashion, privileging enduring quality and craftsmanship. Each item is tended to meticulously, ensuring her presentation is as flawless as it is in honor of her conservative sensibilities.

Her perspective on body image is in harmony with this classic sense of style. The Traditionalist presents herself in a manner that conveys diligent self-care and a refined composure, regardless of her body type. Her physique reflects a devotion to a persona that upholds her values—subtle yet unmistakably dignified.

When it comes to makeup, the Traditionalist opts for the timeless.

A flawless foundation, a stroke of eyeliner, and a swipe of classic red or soft pink lipstick that serve more as a tribute to poise than a pursuit of the spotlight.

Her accessories are chosen with discretion, from the understated elegance of her pearl earrings to the classic lines of her wristwatch. As for hair and nail care, she selects styles that stand the test of time—perhaps a sleek bun or waves gently pinned back. Her nails are impeccably manicured, often in clear or neutral polish, complementing her wardrobe's timeless grace.

- **Keyword:** values
- **Perceived traits:** trustworthy, loyal, organized, practical, consistent, dependable, responsible, reliable, conscientious, appropriate
- **Perceived challenges:** authoritarian, boring, conformist, inflexible, elitist, predictable, reserved, uncreative

The Cosmopolitan: Sophisticated and Eloquent

The Cosmopolitan is an embodiment of luxury and refinement, a sartorial symphony in which each element harmonizes with her sophisticated lifestyle.

Her wardrobe is a subtle murmur of opulence. Designer brands and lavish pieces are selected not merely for their aesthetic allure but also for their ability to broadcast an air of exclusivity and global sophistication. Her wardrobe maintenance mirrors her dedication to a life well-curated, with each garment receiving the meticulous care needed to maintain its premium appearance.

Her view on body image is anchored in elegance. The Cosmopolitan considers her physique as a canvas for high fashion, with each silhouette and contour gracefully adorned in fine materials. The manner in which she carries herself—a synthesis of poise and self-assurance—enhances her impeccable taste in clothing.

When it comes to makeup, she strikes the perfect balance between understated and impactful, crafting a visage that speaks of refinement and luxury.

A perfect base, a hint of color on the cheeks, subtle eye makeup, and a statement lip color that adds just the right touch of sophistication.

Accessories for her are more than adornments; they are declarations of quality and craftsmanship that articulate her discerning preferences.

Her grooming, including hair and nails, follows the philosophy of "less is more"—as long as it's exquisite. Elegant hairstyles that frame her face and a manicure that boasts of subtle, neutral tones or a classic French tip. These choices are intentional, serving not just as aspects of her personal upkeep but as integral parts of her social signature.

Every facet of her appearance, from meticulous skin care routines to the selection of a signature fragrance, is a conscious act in shaping a leadership image that vibrates with the core of high society.

- **Keyword:** quality
- **Perceived traits:** distinguished, proper, notable, cultivated, refined, meticulous, discerning, dignified, excellent
- **Perceived challenges:** arrogant, bossy, calculating, decadent, impersonal, intolerant, stiff, uncaring

Now remember, there is no right or wrong type of primary persona. Each persona, be it the Explorer, Traditionalist, or Cosmopolitan, comes with its unique set of strengths and challenges. Whether you resonate with the unbound spirit of the Explorer, the steadfast resolve of the Traditionalist, or the sophisticated flair of the Cosmopolitan, each brings its distinctive palette of perceived traits and challenges.

If you resonate with the Explorer persona, your inherent approachability and adaptability are tremendous assets in industries such as travel and tourism or outdoor education. Your relatability and hands-on approach can make experiences less intimidating and more enriching, bridging the gap between clients and the natural world they're exploring. In leadership roles in more traditional settings, however, balancing the informal, adventurous spirit of the Explorer with the more conversative executive presence required can be difficult.

For the Traditionalist, your embodiment of trust and reliability lends itself well to fields such as finance, law, or heritage organizations, where tradition and a steady approach are highly valued. Others are drawn to the stability you represent, creating an atmosphere where time-honored practices are appreciated. The challenge may arise in industries that are rapidly innovating, such as technology start-ups, where there's a push for constant evolution and a risk of being seen as outdated.

The Cosmopolitan persona thrives in industries such as luxury brand management, international diplomacy, or high-end hospitality, where quality and a sophisticated professional identity are paramount. Your polished demeanor suits executive roles within these environments. However, oftentimes the challenge is to balance this sophistication with genuine engagement to avoid being misread as aloof, especially in sectors such as human resources or customer service, where a personal touch is crucial.

Yet, remember, your primary persona is the quintessence of your being, the inherent nature you carry from the cradle to the crescendo of your career. It's the unchanging core that defines your authentic self, and it's not something you should attempt to alter.

A Cosmopolitan attempting to mimic the Explorer's casual demeanor, or an Explorer trying to copy the Traditionalist's formality, will often feel uncomfortable, just like an ill-fitting garment.

This incongruence can radiate subtle cues of inauthenticity, leaving others with a sense of dissonance and sensing that something is amiss, even if they can't pinpoint exactly what it is.

Instead, your adaptability comes from your secondary personas—the versatile facets of your identity that you've honed through experience, environment, and personal growth. These are the aspects you can shift and shape to resonate with different people and situations. They enable you to purposefully imprint traits and characteristics onto others, facilitating instant connections without sacrificing the integrity of your true self. These are the facets of your identity that are more fluid, allowing for personal expression and change over time. The four secondary personas are not about changing who you are but about expanding the ways you can authentically interact with the world.

The Caregiver: Supportive and Nurturing

The Caregiver's style resonates with a delicate finesse. These are the women who thread warmth and nurturing into every interaction. In her wardrobe, you'll find fine, small patterns and soft fabrics that offer comfort both to herself and those she encounters. Soft colors such as pastels are prevalent, reflecting her gentle nature and contributing to a calming atmosphere wherever she goes.

Caregivers curate a wardrobe that melds professional expectations with a personal touch. Blouses with delicate lace trims, cardigans in soothing hues, and flowing dresses or skirts exemplify their effortless grace. Her clothing is not merely a uniform but a testament to her role as a nurturer, blending the demands of her profession with innate compassion.

In her body image, the Caregiver appreciates subtlety and health, finding beauty in the natural and the genuine. Her physical presence is characterized by an understated grace, maintaining a physique that speaks to vitality and genuine care rather than vanity.

For the Caregiver, accessories and personal grooming are reflective of her tender approach to life. Jewelry is minimal and meaningful, shoes are chosen for comfort yet display quiet elegance or small embellishments, and grooming is consistent with her overall ethos: thoughtful and impeccably maintained.

When it comes to makeup, she approaches it as she does her role—enhancing features softly and naturally, ensuring her presence is as reassuring as the support she offers. Her hair is often styled in a way that's practical yet inviting, perhaps a soft bun or gentle waves, and her nails are kept clean and neatly polished, often in muted or clear tones.

- **Keyword:** care
- **Perceived traits:** supportive, caring, warm, nurturing, considerate, compassionate, gentle, soft-spoken, receptive, demure
- **Perceived challenges:** anxious, emotional, dependent, insecure, noncompetitive, naïve, passive, undemanding, hesitant

The Avant-Garde: Individualistic and Creative

The Avant-Garde stands as a testament to her creativity and self-expression, valuable in industries that prize innovation, such as interactive media, modern art, or forward-thinking technology sectors. Her appearance is a vibrant tapestry of artistic exploration, with a wardrobe that narrates stories of bold experimentation and the redefining of boundaries.

She selects audacious colors, embraces emerging designers, and favors unique silhouettes that are the hallmarks of her style—a visual celebration of her commitment to pushing the frontiers of fashion. The maintenance of her wardrobe is an act of artistic devotion, each piece cared for with precision or sometimes creatively repurposed in her ongoing narrative.

The Avant-Garde views her physique as a medium for artistic display, embracing a spectrum of styles that challenge conventional beauty norms. She wears her confidence as effortlessly as her eclectic mix of garments, radiating a presence that commands attention and sparks dialogue. She approaches her health with an artistic flair, aligning her physical activities and mental wellness practices with her creative life, even if it means deviating from conventional health routines.

Her accessories, from her statement jewelry to her sculptural shoes, are not mere embellishments but proclamations of her originality, each chosen for its unique design and the conversation it incites.

Her grooming routines are an extension of her creative ethos. Makeup is an opportunity for innovation, and hair and nail care become expressions of her Avant-garde identity, transcending the typical to become part of her artistic statement. Every element of her appearance is a deliberate choice, a chapter in the creative odyssey she embodies, inviting all to witness the living art she presents to the world.

- **Keyword:** creativity
- **Perceived traits:** innovative, imaginative, free-spirited, independent, original, unique, unconventional, fearless, impromptu
- **Perceived challenges:** unrealistic, undisciplined, opinionated, neglectful, inconsistent, disruptive, contrary, awkward

The Glamorous: Magnetic and Extravagant

The Glamorous persona is a paragon of attention and fashion, making her a natural fit for industries such as luxury goods sales, high-end event coordination, or entertainment public relations. Her wardrobe is a bastion of opulence, each piece resonating with the allure of a meticulously curated collection.

Picture her in attire that captivates with its shimmering sequins, reflective sparkles, and a bold color palette—from the fierceness of reds to the solemnity of blacks and the nobility of purples. When it comes to maintaining her wardrobe, she exercises some care, trying to preserve each piece as a cherished element of her sumptuous attire. If it doesn't, no worries, she'll just move on to the next fashion item.

She regards her body as integral to her personal brand; she sculpts her physique to harmonize with her taste and social stature. Her fitness routines are as much a part of her brand narrative as her choice of wardrobe, enhancing her aesthetic and her presence.

Her accessories are selected for their storytelling power and their ability to accentuate her captivating presence. These pieces, however, don't have to be luxurious jewelry or high-end designer shoes. What matters more than the price tag is how much attention the piece can possibly draw to her look.

Her grooming routines are conducted with the same precision and intentionality as dressing for a gala. Makeup for her is artistry, hair care is a discipline, and skin care is a devotion, each facet executed to radiate charisma and draw admiration. This scrupulous cultivation of her appearance reflects a profound appreciation for the transformative power of appearance.

- **Keyword:** attraction
- **Perceived traits:** trendy, stimulating, popular, magnetic, fit, extravagant, daring, attractive, admirable
- **Perceived challenges:** pompous, one-dimensional, manipulative, insincere, indiscreet, flamboyant, deceitful, artificial

The Dramatic: Strong and Fearless

The Dramatic persona is an unforgettable presence, embodying a love for the bold and theatrical that can be harnessed in roles from creative directorships to performance arts management. Her wardrobe is an audacious array of statement pieces that seize attention, mirroring the boldness of her personality.

Her wardrobe is a testament to her fearlessness, with each item chosen for its impact. It's fashion that doesn't just capture the limelight—it generates it, ensuring she isn't just observed but remembered. Architectural collars, oversized sleeves, and other unconventional silhouettes are her staples, each piece a statement in itself. She revels in the strength and sophistication of black, black, and then some more black, allowing it to dominate her wardrobe as the color of her joy. When she opts for other colors, it's strategically employed to forge a stark, memorable contrast that complements her daring sartorial narrative. The maintenance of her wardrobe is as exacting and dramatic as a theater's costume shop: detailed, intentional, and always in pursuit of the remarkable.

She views her body as a stage for a commanding performance. Her confidence is her most treasured garment, enveloping a physique that is as dynamic as her sartorial choices, making a statement as memorable as her own dramatic essence.

Her accessories and beauty routines are essential to her expressive arsenal. Each piece of jewelry, every selection of shoes, and every application of makeup is a thoughtful act of self-expression, adding bold lines to the story she embodies.

For the Dramatic, the world is a vast stage, and she is always in the lead role, with each facet of her appearance carefully curated to etch a lasting impression of her indelible presence in any professional setting.

- **Keyword:** power
- **Perceived traits:** strong, intense, charismatic, demanding, bold, commanding, captivating, aloof, severe, spectacular
- **Perceived challenges:** tough, possessive, intrusive, intense, insensitive, harsh, dominating, cold

It's your secondary persona that allows you to adapt to various roles and environments. Balancing these secondary personas is key to meeting diverse expectations while staying true to your core values. Although balance is crucial, it's important to note that misperceptions often arise when women lean too heavily into the extremes of these personas.

Take the Caregiver, for example. Although the characteristics of empathy, attentiveness, and warmth are crucial traits required for impactful leadership, solely embodying this secondary persona in extremes can lead others to perceive only the caregiver within you. This can overshadow the fact that you also possess qualities such as assertiveness or strategic thinking that might come from your primary persona. These are the women who enter meetings in flowing dresses, with braids in their hair, and cute shoes on their feet—they're the first to organize donuts for the gathering and ask about everyone's family life in a soft-spoken voice. They prioritize harmony in teams and may hesitate to speak up. Then they might face the harsh reality of being stereotyped solely as Caregivers, overlooking their multifaceted abilities. And quite frankly, although the Caregiver is an outstanding persona, it's the one that many women automatically get pigeonholed into based on our stereotyped roles as mothers, nurturers, and caretakers in our society.

Or, consider an Avant-Garde, with her inherent creativity and self-expression, often seen as bold and boundary-pushing in the spectrum of personas. Her daring nature and unconventional approach make her an excellent conduit for embodying traits such as innovation and risk-taking.

However, when your behavior, your communication, and even your visual appearance veer too far into this secondary persona, it can lead to misperceptions. These are the women who may prioritize bold fashion choices, unconventional hairstyles, or extensive makeup looks in professional settings. They're the ones with sticky notes covering their screens and markers coloring their notebooks, the ones who constantly disrupt ideas in meetings with out-of-the-box thinking, sometimes neglecting practicality and execution. Although these traits can be empowering and impactful in certain contexts, being exclusively identified with the Avant-Garde persona might overshadow other valuable aspects of your primary persona, potentially limiting opportunities for recognition and advancement.

Or then there's the Glamorous, the one we all adore and admire for her beauty, the shine she brings into every encounter, the fashion runway she walks on all day long. Yet if these women go too far, they risk being perceived solely for their outer appearance, overshadowing their intelligence, dedication, and hard work. These are the women who may overdo it with their hair, makeup, and attire, opting for excessive glamour, glitter, and skin exposure. Their ensembles may prioritize style over substance, with too much emphasis on appearance. In more traditional settings, their biggest challenge may lie in being exclusively or primarily seen for their outer beauty, leading to misperceptions and missed opportunities for others to discover the smart, dedicated, hard-working woman underneath the glamorous exterior.

And lastly, there's the Dramatic persona, captivating and commanding attention wherever she goes. Although outstanding in situations where a dramatic nature is required, such as on stage or in public communication, when taken to extremes, she risks overshadowing others and being perceived as intimidating or trying too hard. Her powerful behavior and communication style, although effective in some contexts, can come off as cold or competitive, hindering collaboration and rapport-building efforts.

It's essential for her to strike a balance, harnessing her dramatic flair when appropriate while remaining approachable and considerate of others' contributions and perspectives.

As you can see, there is no perfect persona. There's no good or bad; you are uniquely you, and that is perfect. However, it's often when we allow our secondary personas to dominate that they overshadow our true essence—our primary personas. It's about finding harmony and balance within ourselves and embracing all facets of our identity while ensuring that none overshadow the core of who we are. It's about contextually curating your expression to meet the moment and enhancing your authentic self without losing the essence of who you are.

As you continue on your journey, let this understanding guide you. Embrace your primary persona as well as the qualities of your secondary persona to navigate the myriad of expectations you encounter—in your very own, unique, and authentic way.

And should you seek to delve deeper into the fabric of your perceived identity, the end of this book provides a gateway. There, you will find a QR code and a link to a perception persona audit available on my website—a free tool designed to offer insights into which primary or secondary persona you are currently embodying or are perceived as.

Chapter 5
Leaders Look Professional

Strategic Moves to Authority:
Positioning for the End Game.

Chapter 5:
Leaders Look Professional

Navigating the shifting sands of what defines "professional" in today's workplace is an intricate dance, particularly for women. The archetype of professional attire has transcended the era when a crisp suit and conservative accessories demarcated the threshold of leadership and ambition. Today, the concept of looking professional for women is a vibrant tapestry, mirroring the vast expanse of sectors from corporate to nonprofit to education to entrepreneurship and reflecting diverse cultures, generations, and personal styles.

In the past, dress code levels were the compass that directed professional attire for women. These sartorial standards were not just about fashion; they were emblems of seriousness, competence, and intent within a professional context. They also allowed (and still allow) organizations to create a sense of unity and professionalism through a shared visual standard.

From the finesse of boardroom attire to the ease of casual wear, these guidelines provided a narrative for professional presentation. Once the silent custodians of a professional's wardrobe, these dress code levels have now become historical markers, from which the present-day dynamic fashion ethos has emerged.

Let's briefly revisit them, not as the definitive rule book they once were, but as a history lesson from which today's fluid fashion landscape evolved.

Dress code level one: boardroom attire. Boardroom attire was the pinnacle of professional wear, encapsulating formality. Women adorned themselves with classic suits or dresses in dark, commanding hues, paired with pristine white blouses. Skirts maintained a standard of knee-length, and accessories were selected for subtlety—closed-toe pumps, with pantyhose as an indispensable companion, irrespective of the season, and jewelry that whispered of status, such as pearls or fine metals. Hair was often coiffed in a restrained manner, and makeup was applied with a light hand to accentuate a look of natural authority.

Dress code level two: traditional business attire. Traditional business attire offered a broader palette and softer lines. Suits and dresses branched into lighter colors and subtle patterns, whereas blouses could bring a pop of color or a delicate print. Skirts relaxed slightly in fit, and footwear expanded to include colored pumps. Accessories such as scarves could introduce a personal touch, and jewelry might make a bolder statement. Hairstyles softened, and makeup could venture beyond the bare essentials to enhance confidence and presence.

Dress code level three: executive casual. Executive casual introduced an even more personal touch. Blazers paired with slacks or skirts provided a blend of authority and approachability, and the use of fabric and color became more diverse. Open-toed shoes made their debut, and hair and makeup could echo the wearer's personality, offering a palette for more vivid expression. Accessories, now more pronounced, allowed creativity to shine through.

Dress code level four: mainstream casual. Mainstream casual offered a departure from tradition. Blouses gave way to more relaxed tops, even embracing short sleeves for a touch of informality. The color spectrum widened, and patterns became more playful. Footwear could be comfortably chic, reflecting personal style and practicality.

Accessories served as a focal point for individuality, and hair could be more freely styled. Makeup, in harmony with this casual air, could be more experimental.

Dress code level five: baseline casual. Baseline casual was the embodiment of relaxed professionalism. Denim could be polished enough for a casual work setting, provided it was clean and well-fitted. Tops could be comfortable yet remain tasteful, and shoes could range from loafers to tasteful sneakers, as long as they were well-kept. Hair could be worn in a variety of styles that still conveyed intentionality, and makeup could be as understated or as expressive as the overall ensemble allowed. Accessories, although still present, were chosen for comfort and personal expression.

But let's pause now and consider the present. The rules that once dictated professional appearance have been blurred by the evolving landscape of the modern workplace. The once rigid frameworks for leaders have softened, morphing into a more nuanced spectrum of acceptable workwear.

However, the transition toward a more casual wardrobe in many workplaces has introduced a new challenge: whereas the traditional business dress code was meticulously defined, the concept of "casual" remains somehow nebulous and subjective, which often leads to uncertainty and inconsistency.

The integration of diverse cultural norms into the workplace adds another layer of complexity to defining professional or casual dress. With each culture comes a distinct perspective on what constitutes appropriate, which can vary significantly from one to another.

The generational mosaic present in today's workforce further complicates matters. With multiple generations coexisting in the workplace, each brings its own set of attitudes toward self-expression and conformity.

Moreover, the influence of social media and the internet has democratized fashion and trendsetting, often further blurring the lines.

Finally, the pandemic has undeniably reshaped our perceptions as well. The shift to remote work and the adoption of screen-to-screen interactions have introduced a level of informality previously unseen in many sectors.

These factors, combined with the rise of individualism, suggest that the future of attire in the workplace will continue to evolve, prioritizing adaptability and personal expression alongside traditional notions of professionalism. The challenge for today's leaders is to navigate this ever-changing landscape, setting a standard that balances personal authenticity with the expectations of their professional roles.

For women leaders, this involves acknowledging the influence of diverse cultural norms and generational perspectives, understanding the democratization of fashion through social media, and adapting to shifts in work environments catalyzed by factors such as the pandemic.

Professional attire should honor the gravitas of their respective fields, yet be adaptable enough to navigate the modern world's demands. It's about finding that common visual language that respects the tradition of their professions while welcoming the individuality each woman brings to her role.

As we have moved beyond the rigidity of traditional dress code levels, the contemporary professional landscape doesn't hold a one-size-fits-all prescription ready for us that can encompass the myriad of factors influencing a woman's choice of dress in the workplace. The modern professional woman's wardrobe is less about conforming to a strict set of rules and more about crafting a personal dress code that in the best case, performs the following functions:

Bolsters her confidence, making her feel invincible and authentic in her skin, ready to tackle any challenge with the poise of a superhero.

Respects and reflects the environment in which she operates, whether it's the industry nuances, the cultural ethos of her organization, or the expectations tied to her role.

Considers the audience she will encounter, dressing not just for the position she holds but also for the people she serves and collaborates with.

Facilitates versatility, embracing an array of settings and occasions. It's about selecting pieces that can be mixed and matched to suit any engagement or any unexpected encounters she might have throughout the day.

Demonstrates deliberate choices, showing that her attire is a thoughtful component of her professional tool kit.

Pays attention to details, recognizing that grooming, makeup, or the right accessories are the finishing touches to an intentional look.

Invests in quality over quantity, understanding that well-crafted garments are a testament to her professionalism and attention to detail, and the capability to invest in themselves

Balances current trends with classic staples, ensuring her wardrobe remains relevant yet timeless.

Knows the narrative it wants to express, with each garment reflecting a chapter of her personal brand story, aligning her external presentation with her internal values and goals.

Complements, rather than overshadows, her intrinsic talents and abilities, using fashion to accentuate her strengths without causing unnecessary distraction.

Allows her presence to take center stage, with a look that doesn't clamor for attention but supports her personal brand.

Avoids the pitfall of feeling compelled to mirror the traditionally masculine dress of male-dominated spaces, asserting that competence and authority are not monopolized by any gender identity.

Eschews the pressure to dress overly feminine, reinforcing the idea that her value is not predicated on gender norms but on her expertise and contributions.

Embraces trial and error as part of the refinement process, experimenting with new looks and evolving her personal dress code based on feedback and self-reflection.

And lastly, but most importantly, let's reconceptualize a familiar maxim: "Dress for the job you want, not the one you have." Although this adage has merit, I propose a broader perspective to you. Dress not just for the next rung on the career ladder, but with your ultimate objective in mind.

Envision the pinnacle of your career—perhaps it's to become the CEO of a leading firm, an influential policymaker, or an innovator in your field. Whatever your goal, it's vital to begin embodying that role now.

Your wardrobe should be a reflection of your ambition and a projection of your potential. It's about more than the clothes you wear; it's about a consistent expression of your professional identity that aligns with the zenith of your aspirations. Each day is an opportunity to illustrate not just where you are or where you want to be next, but where you are determined to be.

Prescribed Uniformity in Action

In many professions, uniforms are the silent ambassadors of the organization, immediately recognizable symbols that communicate volumes without a word being spoken. They serve as a bridge of trust and authority between the role they have, the person wearing them, and those they serve. Legal and ethical codes are also interwoven into the very fabric of these uniforms, ensuring they adhere to stringent industry standards and safety protocols. They reflect a commitment to upholding the highest professional benchmarks of the field.

In the realm of law enforcement, women adorned with badges and regalia stand as stalwarts of justice and order, embodying the law's might and the community's trust. Their uniform is a bastion of safety, instantly commanding respect and projecting the power vested in their roles.

In military service, the distinct camouflage or dress uniforms worn by women signify honor and discipline. The precise insignia, medals, and ribbons communicate rank, experience, and dedication to service, reflecting an unyielding allegiance to national defense and the collective ethos of their units.

The health care industry embraces uniforms as a symbol of cleanliness and precision. Whether it's the scrubs of a surgical team or the white coats of medical executives, these garments communicate a commitment to care and a readiness to heal. They represent a shared identity rooted in expertise and empathy, central to the healer's covenant with patients and peers alike.

Pilots and flight attendants in the airline industry wear uniforms that reflect precision and professionalism, instilling confidence in travelers. A pilot's crisp uniform signifies not just their ability to navigate the skies but also their leadership in ensuring passengers' safety and comfort.

On the manufacturing floor, the uniform serves a dual purpose: it is both protective gear and an emblem of the collective industrial effort. Women in leadership roles within manufacturing often wear uniforms that resonate with the workforce's attire while distinguishing their supervisory status, signaling an alignment with the production heart of the industry while steering its operations.

These uniforms—be they adorned with stripes, badges, or safety gear—are not simply mandatory attire. They are potent symbols of the roles women have carved out in sectors that are often physically demanding and require decisive leadership. They bridge the gap between individual capability and collective identity, asserting a visual dialogue of expertise and empowerment.

For a woman donning her uniform, it's a mantle of responsibility and an equalizer that underscores her role within a larger team and organization. It is more than fabric and thread—it's a declaration of their commitment.

The relationship between a uniform and the person wearing it is both intimate and public. It can kindle a sense of belonging and purpose, creating an instant visual connection with the public. The uniform is thoughtfully designed to marry necessity with dignity, crafted to allow the wearer to perform their duties with competence and confidence. It accounts for the rigorous demands of the role and the physical needs of the wearer, including practicality, comfort, and safety.

In environments where uniforms are the norm, the scope for personal expression may seem limited, but women can still find creative avenues to infuse their look of leadership. Small, compliant changes can help to add a personal touch. Sometimes the choice of accessories, while remaining within the parameters set by the profession, allows for subtle distinctions. The distinct flair of a tasteful brooch or the understated elegance of a classic leather belt can speak to a woman's personal style without detracting from the uniformity required in her role. A patterned silk scarf or a functional yet stylish timepiece can become signifiers of identity. Where regulations allow, a slight variation in footwear or the style or color of socks or tights can add a discreet touch of personality.

Hairstyles also play a pivotal role. Within the confines of professionalism, hair can be styled to reflect current trends or personal preference, whether it's a sleek bun, a functional pixie cut, or neatly braided hair. Hairpins and bands used to secure styles can be both practical and a reflection of personal taste.

Even the modest addition of a name tag or badge designed with a distinctive font or style can serve as a hallmark of individuality, transforming a generic item into something personal and unique.

These choices, although seemingly minor, can have an impact on how women are perceived and, more importantly, how they perceive themselves within their roles.

Moreover, the meticulous care of a uniform itself—the sharpness of a crease, the precision of a tuck, the cleanliness and crispness of the fabric—can convey a woman's dedication to her role and attention to detail. It is in these meticulously maintained details that individual pride and professionalism shine.

In essence, while the uniform serves to create a cohesive and recognizable entity, the way in which a woman chooses to adorn and maintain it can subtly illuminate her individuality. These thoughtful nuances allow the unique spirit of the woman to permeate the collective identity, honoring the essence of her personality without sacrificing the solidarity of the uniform.

Silent Standards and Unwritten Uniforms

If you think the dialogue on uniforms doesn't apply to your field, it's time to think again. Once again, every industry, every organization, and every role operates within a set of unspoken expectations—silent standards that compose the unwritten uniform of the professional world. These are not codified in employee handbooks, yet they exist in the collective consciousness, guiding judgments and impressions from boardrooms to open-plan offices.

In the world of financial services, for instance, even without a formal mandate, the uniform might include conservative suits, crisp blouses, and subtle accessories.

Or consider a tech start-up, where hoodies, T-shirts, and jeans have become the emblematic garb of innovation and disruptive thinking.

In creative industries such as advertising and design, there's an expectation to embody creativity not just in work but also in appearance. Here, eclectic attire and bold color choices are often the norm, signaling a creative mind at work.

Moving into the public sector, educators are expected to strike a balance between approachable and authoritative, often opting for smart-casual attire that ensures respect while still being relatable to students.

Nonprofit leaders might adopt an approach that blends professionalism with the grassroots essence of their work, often choosing functional and practical clothing that resonates with their mission and the communities they serve.

By decoding these silent standards, women can navigate their industries with a more nuanced understanding of unarticulated yet powerful norms. It's about reading the room, understanding the culture, and dressing in a way that communicates you belong, that you are a credible player in the field, and that you respect the unspoken rules of the game.

But how can you define what your silent uniform should look like?

First, look around. As simple as that. Is there a pattern in the way people (in particular women) dress in your workplace or industry? It's not about mimicking or conforming blindly, but rather understanding the visual language and the nuances that come with it. Take note of the colors, the fits, the levels of formality. Observe the details: the watches, the shoes, the way a scarf is tied, or how a blazer is buttoned. These subtleties are your clues.

Consider the context of your interactions. In client meetings, is there a dominant style? At networking events, what styles stand out and seem to align with success and influence? These are your guideposts. From the boardroom to casual Fridays, each setting has its unwritten dress code that, once deciphered, can be tailored to your advantage.

Reflect on your role within the organization. What are the expectations, spoken and unspoken, for someone in your position? How can your look of leadership showcase your professional strengths and personality without speaking a word? Remember, your silent uniform is not just about fitting in; it's about standing out in the right ways. It's about aligning your external presentation with your career aspirations and the persona you want to project.

Define how far you can integrate your personal touch. Once you understand the silent standards, you can start bending them subtly. It's about finding the balance between industry expectations and your personal style—the sweet spot where your silent uniform empowers you to feel authentic and confident in your professional skin.

Then go back to our preceding exploration of perception personas, as we unveiled the power of keywords—comfort, values, quality, care, creativity, attraction, and power—that anchor the essence of our professional identities. You might encounter your unwritten uniform that speaks to these keywords and the perceived traits they represent. These silent uniforms are not decreed by policy but are ingrained in the fabric of industry expectations and professional culture.

For example, on the one hand, in the high-energy world of a tech start-up, the Explorer archetype with its keyword of comfort and traits of being active and adventurous fits seamlessly. An Explorer's casual and approachable wardrobe aligns perfectly with the innovative and agile atmosphere of such a workplace.

On the other hand, a Traditionalist in this environment might struggle to align their structured, value-driven attire with the casual ethos but could find solace in a corporate culture that values organization and dependability.

Or, consider the Cosmopolitan in the world of luxury brands or high finance—industries where quality, distinction, and refinement are not just appreciated but expected. Their meticulous and cultivated attire sends a powerful message of discernment and propriety that resonates well with the industry's and role's elevated standards. Conversely, an Explorer navigating the polished corridors of luxury brands or the buttoned-up world of high finance might feel constrained.

Or, in the world of education, the Caregiver persona might find fertile ground because the traits of support and warmth are integral to nurturing young minds. The gentle and nurturing disposition of the Caregiver is perfectly suited to this setting, where their attire can be both functional and infused with compassion. The Caregiver's presence, often accented with a smile or a kindly gesture, aligns with the educational ethos of patience and guidance. However, a Dramatic persona in this same environment might face challenges. The dramatic flair—characterized by boldness and a commanding nature—may need to be moderated to foster the nurturing and secure atmosphere that primary education so deeply values.

Does this mean you need to overhaul and change your perception persona to fully match the uniform your industry, corporate culture, or profession expect? No. By no means.

However, this understanding might elucidate why, in certain contexts, you feel like a seamless part of the tapestry, whereas in others you feel like you stand out without being able to pinpoint the reason. It's not about altering your core identity; rather, it's about fine-tuning the following characteristics.

Balancing personas: Everyone has a primary persona and one or more secondary personas. It's about leveraging this spectrum appropriately. For instance, your Caregiver qualities may be front and center in a nurturing role, whereas your secondary Avant-garde traits can come into play when innovation is called for. Balancing personas is about the strategic interplay between different facets of your character. It recognizes that a woman is not one-dimensional—she can be nurturing and innovative, methodical and creative, all at once. By emphasizing certain traits in specific contexts, you can align your leadership image with your role's expectations while maintaining your unique essence. This alignment enhances your relatability and effectiveness, allowing you to connect with colleagues and clients on multiple levels and in a variety of scenarios.

Borrowing elements: This is about selectively adopting characteristics from other personas that resonate with your personal style. A Glamorous persona might borrow small elements from the Cosmopolitan's flair for quality for a high-stakes business meeting, or a Traditionalist could take on a nuance from the Caregiver's warm approach for a team-building retreat. Borrowing elements involves curating aspects from other personas to complement one's dominant traits. This selective synthesis creates a dynamic professional persona that can adapt and thrive across a range of settings. It's about enriching your personal narrative by integrating diverse qualities that broaden your appeal and enhance your influence. This nuanced approach enables a woman to be perceived as multifaceted and versatile, showcasing her ability to evolve and respond to different professional challenges.

Certainly, you can also choose to disrupt these patterns of unspoken uniforms. History is punctuated with stories of women who have shattered expectations and redefined the norms of their industries, becoming icons of success on their own terms and with their own looks.

They are trailblazers, the rare exceptions who prove that rules can be broken with the right combination of timing, talent, and tenacity.

Yet, it is crucial to acknowledge that these cases are exceptional for a reason—they stand out against a backdrop of more typical narratives. For every convention-defying success story, there are countless others who navigate the intricate dance of expectations and self-expression with more subtlety. The most common pathway to success often involves aligning with the established norms while finding small but significant ways to showcase individuality.

The decision, ultimately, is deeply personal. It's about weighing the potential benefits of fully disrupting the existent norm or standing out step-by-step. It's about understanding not just who you are, but how best to convey that identity in a way that resonates within your professional context. This is not about surrendering to the status quo, but about making informed choices.

Your career, your professional identity, your persona—these are yours to define. Whether you choose to align with silent standards or set your course, your look of leadership can be a powerful tool in your professional arsenal. Use it with purpose, with insight, and most importantly, with a clear vision of the outcome you desire. The silent uniform of your industry or role doesn't need to be a straitjacket; it can be a canvas—sometimes for blending in, sometimes for standing out. The art is in knowing when to do which, and the wisdom is in recognizing the choice is always, unequivocally, yours.

Internal Mandates We Self-Enforce

These include the choices you self-enforce on yourself. Yes, you heard that right. Many of us are guilty of setting unwritten rules for ourselves, internal guidelines we adhere to—often unconsciously—that shape our professional identity and wardrobe.

These self-imposed standards can be as binding as any corporate dress code, yet they stem not from a company policy but from our own insecurities, and the societal expectations we've absorbed over time.

This self-enforcement can manifest in numerous ways, subtly dictating our choices. It's the invisible uniform we design ourselves, woven from the threads of the "shoulds" and "musts" we've collected throughout our personal and professional lives. They are the mental garments made up of beliefs about how we need to appear to be accepted, respected, and successful.

It's time to take a closer look at the expectations some of us have built for ourselves. Let's unfold a few of them below.

Conforming to masculine dress codes is a notion deeply rooted in the historical context of the workplace. For decades, power and authority in professional settings have been visually represented by masculine attire—sharp suits, strict silhouettes, and muted colors. As women entered male-dominated fields, the prevailing belief was that to succeed, one must assimilate, which often meant mirroring the look of their male counterparts. However, this approach is becoming outdated and is not recommended.

First, it can suppress your unique identity, compelling you to fit into an aesthetic that may not resonate with your personal style or the full breadth of your professional capabilities. If the masculine attire feels inauthentic to you, it can affect your confidence and performance. Remember, your clothing is not just fabric; it's psychological armor. When you dress in ways that make you feel strong and genuine, your mindset and actions tend to match that authenticity. If you do the opposite, well, then you encourage the opposite result.

Second, this notion might unintentionally uphold the very gender biases that many sectors are striving to overcome. It implies that to be a leader, you must downplay feminine attributes.

If you equate a masculine appearance with professionalism, it risks negating the diverse ways in which women can express their executive presence. You can help redefine the norms, broadening what it means to dress like a leader.

Furthermore, it may actually backfire, creating a perception of overcompensation. This could lead to judgments of trying too hard to fit into the "boys' club," a perception that can emanate from all gender identities, potentially even your own.

So, instead, I encourage you to choose a look that reflects your professional identity and personal style, allowing a richer expression of leadership. This is not about clothes overshadowing capability; rather, it's about reinforcing that authority and professionalism are defined by your actions and knowledge, not the cut of your jacket or the color of your blouse.

Dressing in an overly feminine manner to emphasize gender identity can also be a nuanced issue within the professional realm. For you as a leader, the inclination to overaccentuate femininity with clothing that's decidedly more ornate, or with beauty routines that are exceptionally elaborate, might stem from a desire to assert your identity in a workplace that's traditionally not recognized for its gender diversity. It can be an attempt to reclaim the narrative of femininity in spaces where it has been undervalued or overlooked.

However, just as adopting a predominantly masculine wardrobe can have its pitfalls, so too can an excessively feminine presentation. It risks diverting attention from your competence to your appearance, overshadowing your professional expertise with personal aesthetics. The silent but potent subtext is that your professional value is intertwined with conventional beauty standards, which can undermine the respect you command based on your merit and accomplishments.

The reality is that your leadership is defined by the intellect, emotional intelligence, and experience you bring to the table.

So, although there's power in embracing and expressing your femininity, it's crucial to find a balance that doesn't tip into the realm of excess—be it through overtly ornate attire, intense grooming rituals, or an abundance of accessories. The key is to strike a harmonious chord between asserting your gender identity and underscoring your professional identity. Your goal should be to be acknowledged for your leadership acumen and contributions, not solely for the femininity you express through your wardrobe or beauty choices. You should aim for a presentation that affirms your womanhood without allowing it to overshadow the multifaceted woman and leader you are.

Prioritizing others' needs over your own often goes hand in hand with minimizing attention on oneself or personal expenses. This self-enforced austerity can emerge from a place of nurturance—placing the needs of family, colleagues, your community, or the role you serve above your own. It reflects a commendable selflessness but can inadvertently lead to self-neglect.

Maybe you too may have found yourself allocating resources—time, money, and energy—to support and uplift others, even if it means your professional wardrobe takes a backseat. However, this can result in a professional identity, including your wardrobe, that doesn't reflect your status or ambition, possibly affecting how you're perceived by peers and subordinates. There's a fine line between being resourceful and neglecting or underselling yourself.

Simultaneously, by consistently limiting your expenditure for yourself, you might unwittingly signal you don't value yourself or your role as much as you should. Although fiscal prudence is a virtue, it's also important to recognize that investing in your professional attire is not mere vanity—it's an integral part of personal branding and asserting your professional presence.

The goal is to achieve a balance where caring for others doesn't come at the expense of neglecting your needs. This is not about extravagance but about making considered choices that empower you.

Recognize that you can be a caregiver and a leader while still honoring your personal and professional requirements. Allow yourself permission to invest in your appearance to make you feel confident and capable, reflecting the leader you truly are. It's about self-respect as much as it's about practicality and projecting a leadership image that aligns with your professional aspirations.

Holding on to the belief that what has worked for years will continue to serve you well can be another pitfall, especially regarding your wardrobe. For yourself, it might reinforce a mindset that undervalues your personal and professional progress and self-worth, potentially leading to stagnation in both self-image and career development. Others might perceive this as a reluctance to adapt to new phases of a career or even interpret it as a lack of investment in one's professional growth. In the workplace, where visual cues often communicate ambition and dynamism, an unchanging appearance could mistakenly signal complacency or lack of innovation. On the contrary, periodically updating your professional attire can signal to colleagues and external partners alike that you are evolving, attuned to the present, and investing in your career journey. No, this is not about the pursuit of every fleeting trend, nor is it dismissing the value of timeless statement pieces that anchor a wardrobe. However, when years turn into a decade with the same, unaltered look, it may be time to acknowledge that your sartorial choices are speaking volumes. Updating your look of leadership isn't frivolity—it's a strategic refresh, signaling your continued relevance and evolution in your career and beyond.

Struggling with an "age-appropriate" look is a tug-of-war that spans the spectrum of women's professional lives. As a leader, you might wrestle with the expectation of dressing in a way that aligns with perceived age norms—being trendy and youthful, or reserved and mature.

This self-imposed standard can be confining, often leading to a wardrobe that feels out of sync with your personal identity and professional acumen.

Younger women may feel the need to dress older to garner respect and authority, whereas older women might dress younger to maintain a veneer of vitality and relevance. This pendulum swing between dressing older or younger to meet external expectations underscores a deeper issue—conformity to age norms as a perceived prerequisite for professional acceptance.

The challenge lies in transcending these societal dictates that attempt to define what is suitable for various ages within professional contexts. Such constraints can dilute your individuality and inadvertently signal messages about your currency in the workplace that are misaligned with your actual contributions.

Moreover, this concern with age extends beyond the wardrobe into the realm of cosmetic alterations. In a society that both venerates youth and respects the wisdom of age, some women turn to plastic surgery and others to aesthetic procedures. When chosen from a place of self-love and as an empowerment tool, these changes can indeed bolster self-esteem and personal satisfaction.

However, when taken to the extreme, one must ponder the message being sent. Overemphasis on youth through extensive surgery can suggest a reluctance to embrace the natural aging process, which is as much a part of life as the experience that accrues with it. It can raise questions about the value placed on appearance versus the wealth of knowledge and expertise acquired over a career.

In crafting your professional identity, whether through clothes or alterations, the aim should not be to camouflage your age but to celebrate the individual you have become at every stage of your journey. Authenticity in how you present yourself—acknowledging that every wrinkle has been earned and every fresh perspective is valuable—can resonate more deeply than any attempt to conform to narrow age expectations.

Limiting self-expression in professional settings is a self-limiting belief often rooted in deep-seated cultural, familial, and societal norms. You might find yourself trying hard to blend in, to choose the muted colors, the conservative cuts, and the subdued accessories that won't rock the boat. It's a learned behavior—ingrained from early on by well-meaning advice, observations of family members conforming to their own workplaces, or cultural narratives that prize conformity over individuality.

This limitation can become a barrier to showcasing the full richness of your personality and professional potential. You may feel compelled to downplay your unique flair or stifle the creative impulse in your choice of clothing because standing out is equated with standing apart—and not always in a good way.

However, this inclination to blend in fails to recognize the power and importance of personal branding in today's professional landscape. Authentic self-expression through clothes is not just about fashion—it's a form of nonverbal communication that can speak volumes about your confidence, creativity, and leadership style. It's about striking a balance between respecting workplace decorum and embracing the distinctive qualities that set you apart.

By gently pushing against these inherited boundaries of self-expression, you open the door to a wardrobe that's not just acceptable, but also memorable and true to who you are. It's a delicate process of testing the waters, of gradually introducing elements of personal style into your professional look, and of realizing your individuality can be a professional asset, not a liability.

Remember, the goal is not to disregard the influence of family, culture, or tradition but to evolve these influences into a personal style that complements your professional journey. You're not rewriting the narrative you've been given; you're expanding it to include your unique chapters. It's about allowing yourself to shine within the framework of your professional environment, contributing your voice to the chorus in a way that is harmoniously yours.

Assuming the "perfection" burden is another self-imposed standard where you believe that every aspect of your appearance needs to be flawless. This pursuit of perfection in how your dress sits, how your hair falls, or how your makeup is applied can become an exhaustive endeavor. Rooted in the idea that to be taken seriously, to be deemed competent, or to be respected, one must present a leadership image free of any perceived faults, this belief places immense pressure on you to maintain an impeccable facade at all times. This burden, however, is not just about the external effort to appear polished; it's often deeply intertwined with your own fear of judgment and the desire for acceptance. The constant vigilance over your appearance can lead to heightened anxiety and a critical self-view, where every minor wrinkle or misplaced hair is seen as a potential flaw that could undermine your professional credibility.

Yet, the quest for perfection is a Sisyphean task. Not only is it unattainable, but also it obscures the truth that authenticity and relatability are often more compelling than flawlessness. The most respected leaders are those who present themselves as human—approachable, genuine, and capable of embracing their imperfections.

Releasing yourself from the perfection burden doesn't mean abandoning self-care or professionalism; rather, it's about redefining what those concepts mean to you. It's about allowing yourself the grace to accept minor imperfections and recognizing that your value as a woman is not solely contingent on an immaculate appearance. This shift in perspective can liberate you from the cycle of over-scrutiny, reducing anxiety and fostering a more confident, authentic professional presence.

These are just a few of the self-limiting standards some of us might impose upon ourselves, shadow uniforms that can unconsciously shape our professional journey.

However, it's crucial to always remember that your value in the workplace extends far beyond the confines of your visual appearance or the perfection of your presentation.

Your expertise, your insights, and your contributions cannot be diminished by the superficial. Only in recognizing and challenging these self-imposed barriers can you grant yourself the freedom to express your professional identity more confidently.

Dressing Beyond the Code: Situational Awareness

In the diverse terrain of modern leadership, where the look of leadership can swing from boardroom formal to start-up casual, the concept of situational awareness is not just beneficial—it's imperative. Understanding the nuances of each context means you can navigate spaces with the acumen your role demands. It's about reading the room or the moment and adapting your appearance accordingly, which in turn communicates your agility and attunement to the subtleties of the situation.

Situational awareness speaks to the ability to discern what is appropriate beyond written dress codes, industry norms, or even the personal standards you may set for yourself. It's recognizing there are occasions when the usual rules do not apply and a different approach is called for—one that aligns with the unique dynamics of the current environment or event.

There will be times when the rigidity of formal clothes may be counterproductive, just as there will be moments when overly casual wear might undermine the gravity of your role.

Situational awareness is the compass that guides you through these decisions, ensuring that your look contributes positively to the narrative of your leadership. It allows you to embody the versatility that is increasingly required of leaders today—not just in thought and action, but in the visual rhetoric of your professional presence. Hence, at times, for example, you'll need to . . .

Consider times of crisis or significant organizational change, where leaders may forgo traditional business outfits for something that reflects solidarity with their team and adaptability. In such scenarios it's less about form and more about symbolism and pragmatism. Think of company restructuring or mergers, a product recall or a critical project phase, or worldwide crises or a natural disaster. In such instances, choosing a look that is practical, durable, and less formal is crucial. These choices, intentional and considerate, signal that you're fully engaged and empathetic to the challenges at hand. It's about rolling up your sleeves, both metaphorically and literally, to lead with empathy and readiness—emphasizing that leadership isn't just about directing from above but about being right there with your team.

Accept that practicality can beat professionalism or personal style. Because, in the diverse environments that define our work, practical considerations often have to influence our look of leadership. As a speaker at a conference under the glaring focus of the stage lights, you're compelled to select clothes that won't clash with the technology around you. Your clothing should be amenable to the microphones, the lights, and the movement across the stage, just as your makeup should be a touch more dramatic to ensure your expressiveness translates across the room.

Similarly, if you are a leader in manufacturing, when you step out from your corporate office to visit a construction site, you may need to adapt your attire not just to ensure safety and practicality but to exemplify you understand the circumstances and environment your team members work in.

In these situations, your look of leadership is not just about looking the part but about facilitating the part. They serve as reminders that sometimes practicality must take the stage over professional polish or personal style. It is in these moments your look becomes a tool of the trade that is integral to the performance of professional duties.

Understand that you are a leader at all times, not just during business hours. This omnipresent leadership means that perception is continuous, and the silent dialogue of your visual appearance is always engaged. You need to remember you are a visible symbol of someone in a position of influence of your organization, industry, or personal brand 24/7/365.

Even in the absence of direct reports or colleagues, your look of leadership should always subtly communicate your role and readiness for engagement.

This means at a coffee shop where a chance encounter with a potential client or partner could occur, your choice of outfit should bridge the gap between personal downtime and professional readiness. On the plane when you are headed to your next conference to attend, one of the potential sponsors could be evaluating your appearance before you even had a chance to speak with them. While volunteering, whether for a cause related to your industry or something personal, your clothes again speak to your commitment to leadership and community. Even in the digital realm, your leadership is constantly on display. How you present yourself in video calls from home or in your profile picture on professional networking sites should always reflect the consistency of your professional identity.

In all these contexts, it's not necessarily about donning a suit or formal wear, but about embodying the essence of leadership in your presentation. It's about the strategic selection of clothing that feels authentic to you while also respecting the perception of leadership that you've cultivated. This conscious curation of your out-of-office look of leadership is a testament to the perpetual nature of your professional identity.

Instill this concept within your team, because as the woman at the helm, it's also part of your role to guide your team in understanding this concept. It's about encouraging them to consider their visual appearance as an extension of their professional presence, no matter the setting.

You need to foster an understanding that even when the tie comes off or the heels are swapped for flats, there's a level of consideration that goes into how each team member reflects the shared identity of your company—always and anywhere.

Your leadership in this aspect sets the tone. Your choices signal to your team that professional presence doesn't fluctuate with the clock but is a constant, ingrained in the very fabric of who you are as a professional collective. Thus, in guiding your team in these nuances, you reinforce the brand and reputation of your organization, strengthening public confidence not just in individual leaders but also in the collective identity of the company you represent. It's a powerful testament to the idea that great leadership is omnipresent, influencing and inspiring at every opportunity.

Chapter 6
Leaders Look Respectful

Failing to Respect Yourself Casts Doubt on Your Ability to Respect Others.

Chapter 6:
Leaders Look Respectful

The concept of respect is foundational in any sphere, and in any women's leadership work it's a cornerstone that cannot be overstressed. It's the glue that not only binds together the strands of integrity, credibility, and authority in a leader's tapestry but also bridges the gap between traditional expectations and modern leadership paradigms. Respect is a multifaceted gem that particularly reflects women leaders' regard for themselves, their positions, their teams, and the collective ethos of the organizations they steer.

For women in leadership, respect extends beyond mere professional courtesy. It's a profound acknowledgment of the unique challenges and triumphs that define their journey. It's an unwavering commitment to upholding the highest standards of integrity and excellence, even in the face of bias or adversity. It's a daily practice of honoring the trust placed in them by those they lead and those they serve.

Respect is also about recognizing and celebrating the diverse strengths and perspectives that women bring to the leadership table. It's about creating an inclusive environment where every voice is heard and every contribution is valued. When women leaders embody respect in their words and actions, they set a powerful example for their teams and their organizations. They inspire others to rise to their highest potential and to work together towards a common purpose.

For women in leadership, dressing with respect is a nuanced dance between expressing individuality and honoring the mantle of their roles. It articulates values and sets a tone for interactions, speaking volumes before a word is even uttered. When women choose a look of leadership that resonates with respect, they make a statement about their personal standards and their dedication to their roles. It's a visible manifestation of self-regard and a sophisticated acknowledgment of the responsibility they carry.

However, the flip side—a lack of respect—can acutely undermine a woman leader's authority. It risks perpetuating outdated stereotypes, eroding trust, and creating an atmosphere that influences the broader organizational culture. Such lapses can lead to diminished morale, reduced influence, and lost opportunities.

Respect in leadership is not just about how others perceive a woman leader, but also about how she perceives herself. It's about cultivating a deep sense of self-worth and self-confidence that radiates outward and inspires others to believe in her vision and follow her lead. When a woman respects herself, she sets a powerful example for her team and her organization. She demonstrates that true leadership comes from within, and that it's rooted in a strong sense of purpose to making a positive impact.

Respect is not a one-way street; it's reciprocal. As a woman, when you show respect for yourself through your look of leadership, you set a standard. You are more likely to garner respect in return, cultivating a professional environment where mutual respect flourishes. This mutual acknowledgment is essential for forging strong, productive relationships and establishing an empowering workplace dynamic that supports both individual and collective aspirations.

Moreover, respect in leadership is about recognizing and valuing the unique contributions of each team member. It's about creating a culture of inclusivity and belonging, where everyone feels seen, heard, and appreciated for who they are and what they bring to the table.

When women leaders prioritize respect in their interactions and decision-making, they foster a sense of trust and collaboration that drives innovation, creativity, and success.

It's a visual testament to your dedication to your profession and to those you lead. Whether in the corporate boardroom, the nonprofit sphere, the educational domain, or elsewhere, your respectful look can reinforce an atmosphere of professionalism and assurance, or detract from it. It can acknowledge the trust placed in you by your managers, colleagues, team members, clients, and stakeholders, and it can enforce the perception that you are considerate about the various cultural or organizational norms and expectations of those you are leading or seeking to influence. It illustrates that for you a respectful look of leadership is not merely about fabric and trends but a silent, potent conduit of communication and command.

At its core, respect in leadership is about embodying the values and principles that define your organization and your profession. It's about setting the tone for how people interact with each other, how they approach their work, and how they represent themselves to the world. When women leaders prioritize respect, they create a ripple effect that touches every aspect of their organization and beyond.

It's a Sign of Self-Respect

Self-respect is not about displaying self-importance but rather a profound acknowledgment of one's worth and capabilities. It manifests in the meticulous care you take in your appearance, reflecting an inner ethos of precision and attention to detail that's critical in your role. Self-respect is also about being true to oneself and one's values, even in the face of adversity or criticism. It's about having the courage to stand up for what you believe in, even when it's not popular or easy. When women leaders demonstrate self-respect through their words and actions, they inspire others to do the same.

They create a culture of authenticity and integrity that is essential for building trust and fostering long-term success.

Moreover, self-respect is about setting healthy boundaries and prioritizing self-care. It's about recognizing that leadership is not about sacrificing one's own well-being for the sake of the organization, but rather about leading by example and modeling a balanced, fulfilling life. When women leaders respect themselves enough to prioritize their own needs and desires, they create a more sustainable and resilient leadership style that benefits everyone.

It's the executive whose attire is impeccable, signaling respect for the sanctity of her position. It's the entrepreneur whose ensemble is thoughtfully curated, showcasing commitment to her brand. It's the educator whose professional dress underlines the seriousness with which she approaches her influence on future generations. Their self-respect is evident in the quality of the materials, the fit of the garments, and the choice of accessories that, although perhaps subtle, make a definitive statement.

Dressing with self-respect is not merely about the price tag or the label—but remember, being willing to invest in yourself is also a sign of self-respect. It's also about selecting attire that fits well, is appropriate for the myriad of roles you fulfill, and is maintained with care. At its core, it's about ensuring your wardrobe is curated with the same precision and consideration as your work, with each piece a chapter in the story of your professional journey.

This level of self-respect should not diminish at the close of business hours but should persist as a constant in every aspect of life. This armor of self-respect is not about vanity or superficiality; it represents the pride that comes from presenting your best self in every scenario, personal and professional.

Self-respect is also about embracing one's unique identity and celebrating the qualities that make you who you are. It's about owning your strengths and weaknesses, your successes and failures, and using them as fuel for growth and learning.

When women leaders approach their roles with a deep sense of self-respect, they bring their whole selves to the table. They lead with authenticity, vulnerability, and courage, inspiring others to do the same.

Investing in yourself and treating yourself respectfully transcends mere aesthetics; it is a daily ritual of arming yourself for the day's challenges and opportunities. It reflects readiness to lead and an appreciation of the weight of your responsibilities. And this might require not just time but also financial investment. Again, this is not to suggest extravagance; rather, it is about securing the best you can afford within your means.

Moreover, it will set a benchmark for your team. By leading with such an example, you demonstrate that you value not only your role but also the individuals you lead. Leaders who embody this level of self-respect engender confidence and spur their teams to also take pride in their professional presentation. This cyclic reinforcement of respect is what propels a team from functioning to excelling in their pursuit of excellence.

It Shows That You Respect Others

For women in leadership, demonstrating respect through your visual appearance is a profound nod to the trust placed in them by their teams, clients, and partners. Your careful curation of a look of leadership is a message that you honor the workplace environment and its nuances. It reassures those you lead that their careers, contributions, and welfare are in the hands of someone who appreciates the gravity of their collective efforts.

Respecting others in leadership also means being mindful of the power dynamics at play and using one's influence for good. It's about creating an environment where everyone feels safe to speak up, share ideas, and challenge the status quo. When women leaders demonstrate respect for others through their actions and decisions, they foster a culture of psychological safety that is essential for innovation and growth.

This also means being an advocate and ally for those who may be underrepresented or marginalized. It's about using one's platform and privilege to amplify diverse voices and perspectives, and to create opportunities for everyone to thrive. When women leaders prioritize respect and inclusivity in their approach, they build stronger, more resilient teams and organizations.

The corporate world is also a microcosm of diverse cultures, genders, and generations. Each meeting, presentation, or corporate event is an opportunity to show esteem for these differences. Choosing wardrobe items that are sensitive to cultural norms sidesteps clichés and maintains a professional standard, and you broadcast a deep-seated respect for the multifaceted identities within your network.

Subtlety and appropriateness are your allies in this endeavor. It's about striking the delicate balance between expressing personal style and embodying the ethos of leadership—a balance that, when achieved, fosters a culture of respect and elevates the entire professional landscape.

Avoiding distraction in your outfits and personal grooming choices is crucial in crafting a professional identity that respects others and aligns with the demands of leadership across fields. For you as a leader, this avoidance of distraction is a silent contract with those you lead, assuring them that your focus is unwavering, your commitment is absolute, and your dedication to excellence and progress is paramount.

Respect is the foundation upon which effective leadership is built. For women in leadership, demonstrating respect through their appearance, actions, and decisions is a powerful way to set the tone for their organizations and inspire others to rise to their highest potential. As we navigate the complexities of the modern workplace, let us remember that respect is not just a nice-to-have, but a critical component of successful leadership.

Chapter 7
Leaders Look Controlled

The More You Control,
the Better the Outcome.

Chapter 7:
Leaders Look Controlled

The ability to strategize or innovate is an essential part of women's leadership, and it profoundly influences women's professional identity. The tapestry of how she is perceived is intricate, demanding each piece be positioned with intention. This art of self-presentation, where every choice from clothing to communication style is a deliberate act, constructs the comprehensive professional identity of her as a leader in the eyes of the world.

Envision your leadership image as a continual curation of your professional persona. Every detail, from the subtlety of your accessories to the precision of your clothing, is a declaration of the control you possess over your personal and professional narrative. It's a powerful statement that says, "I am the author of my fate; I steer the course of my success," and it speaks volumes about your self-assurance and the respect you command—silently yet resoundingly.

You, as a woman guiding others, take the reins of your professional identity not by chance but through a disciplined routine that echoes your professional diligence. You know that although not every perception can be influenced, to neglect consciously crafting your leadership image is to allow others to sketch in the blanks, often with incongruent strokes. Thus, intentionally shaping your narrative ensures that it remains firmly in your hands, a true reflection of your ability to guide not only your own path but also the trajectory of those who follow your lead.

Taking control of your professional identity is not an act of vanity but rather a strategic move. It's an affirmation that even though you can't control every perception, you can certainly lay a solid, indelible foundation that resonates with the identity you aim to project.

Why leave such a powerful aspect to serendipity? Why permit happenstance to dictate what can be shaped with purpose and precision?

Women who leave indelible marks are those who wield their professional identity as a vibrant and influential facet of their leadership repertoire. They choose their wardrobe, they mind their grooming, and they conduct themselves not solely for style but for the substantive legacy they're building. They are the ones who seize the narrative, orchestrating not only their strategic boardroom presence but also the unspoken stories evoked by their demeanor.

Like a skilled CEO who strategizes and executes each business move with precision and foresight, as a woman in leadership, you must embrace every tool at your disposal. Your career is a tapestry of roles and achievements, yes, but also of the conscious effort to sculpt your professional identity with intention. This process is a cycle of:

- **self-awareness,** where reflection becomes as routine as strategy meetings;

- **self-care,** where discipline in personal presentation is akin to financial stewardship; and

- **self-promotion,** where advocating for your achievements is as crucial as marketing your organization's successes.

In cultivating your professional identity with such intention and consideration, you do more than advance your career trajectory—you lay down a pathway for excellence.

Self-Awareness and Self-Reflection

Self-awareness and self-reflection are pillars of professional growth and leadership, crucial for women who are forging their paths in various sectors. This introspective journey starts with a deep dive into one's strengths, vulnerabilities, and core values, as well as an honest assessment of the effect one has on others in the workplace and the broader business environment or community.

This process is about continuous inward exploration, challenging oneself with difficult questions about motives and unconscious biases, and the ripple effects of one's decisions. It means pausing after each significant event to evaluate successes and missteps, fostering a culture of perpetual learning and self-improvement. Such reflection is indispensable in the dynamic, high-stakes scenarios that women leaders frequently navigate, offering a means to evolve from every experience.

Beyond personal reflection, self-awareness for women in leadership means understanding how their professional identity influences their organization's culture. It's about recognizing the pivotal role they play within their teams, how their leadership style affects team cohesion, and how their strategic decisions drive the organization's progress and success.

This self-awareness should profoundly shape your look of leadership, guiding you to cultivate a visual appearance that is congruent with your role and values and the expectations of those who look to you for guidance. Contemplating your visual presentation is far from superficial—it is a strategic consideration of how your appearance can affirm or undermine perceptions of your competence, approachability, and professionalism. This includes considering the messages sent by certain styles, colors, fabrics, patterns, or levels of formality. It involves asking yourself questions such as "Does my attire convey the authority and expertise expected of my role?" or "Is my appearance accessible and reassuring to people from diverse backgrounds?" or "How does my personal style affect my team's perception of my leadership?"

As a woman in leadership, the way you present yourself should answer these questions and mirror your core principles. It's about deciding to wear clothing that doesn't just fit the body but fits the moment and the mission. Your look of leadership should communicate that you're grounded in expertise, yet your feet walk the same ground as those you're leading. It's in the way your professionalism doesn't overshadow your humanity—it accentuates it.

Self-Care and Self-Discipline

Self-care and self-discipline stand as crucial supports for both personal well-being and professional prowess. For women in leadership, self-care often takes on an added layer of significance. It's about nurturing your physical, emotional, and mental health, which is especially important given the tendency for women to prioritize the care of others—often at the expense of their own well-being.

It's no secret that the ingrained focus on caretaking can make it difficult for women to turn the lens of care inward. Yet, just as the familiar airline safety instruction advises us to secure our own oxygen masks before assisting others, self-care for you operates on the same principle: if you neglect your own well-being, it will manifest in your ability to lead. To be seen as capable of nurturing and guiding others, you must visibly take care of yourself first.

This isn't about self-indulgence but about fundamental maintenance that enables effective leadership. It's a clear signal to your team and peers that you are well-prepared to manage the multifaceted demands of leadership. It communicates that you understand the importance of balance and are equipped to handle the various responsibilities and individuals who rely on your guidance and expertise.

Discipline is the commitment to maintaining these self-care practices regularly and making choices that align with your long-term goals and values, even when they require sacrifice or delay of gratification. This includes a broad spectrum of habits that keep you at your best—be it through adequate sleep, nutritious eating, physical activity, or mindfulness practices. These activities are not luxuries but necessities that enable you to perform at your peak.

Discipline, especially in the context of self-care, also involves setting boundaries to protect your time and energy. It means being able to say no to nonessential demands and recognizing when you need to step back and recharge. It not only prevents burnout but also models healthy behavior for your team members, reinforcing the importance of well-being in sustaining high performance.

However, the irony lies in the fact that although discipline may not be a struggle in its application to external tasks, there is a nuanced challenge in turning that discipline inward. It's a nuanced imbalance where the rigor applied to caring for others isn't always matched by the discipline needed for self-nourishment and rejuvenation. Acknowledging and addressing this imbalance is crucial, for disciplined self-care is the reservoir from which the strength to lead others is drawn. Only when leaders apply the same level of discipline to their own well-being as they do to their professional duties can they truly embody the comprehensive excellence that leadership demands.

This doesn't demand perfection or a stringent adherence to unrealistic standards of professional identity. Rather, it's about crafting a presence that reflects the seriousness with which you approach your responsibilities and the trust placed in you.

Self-Improvement and Self-Promotion

In the vibrant realm of leadership, continuous self-improvement and strategic self-promotion underscore the ever-evolving journey of personal and professional growth. As the CEO of your own career, embracing self-improvement means recognizing that the pursuit of excellence has no end. It is a commitment to ongoing education, skill refinement, and personal evolution.

At the same time, self-promotion, which is often misunderstood and can carry a stigma of self-aggrandizement, is actually a vital component of leadership. It's about articulating and celebrating your achievements, not out of vanity but as a powerful form of advocacy for the value you bring to your organization. It involves illuminating your contributions in a manner that fosters recognition and serves as a beacon for others. This approach not only paves the way for your own advancement but also raises the profile of your team's efforts, aligning with and advancing the collective objectives of your company or industry.

Self-promotion for many women leaders can be an intricate challenge, partly rooted in societal expectations and gender norms. Historically, women have been encouraged to be collaborative and communal rather than assertive and self-promoting, leading to an internal conflict for many of us when it comes time to highlight one's own accomplishments. Many women grapple with the fine line between being perceived as confident and being labeled as self-important. They worry that by asserting their achievements, they may encounter backlash. This concern is compounded by the imposter syndrome that many high-achieving women experience, where despite their accomplishments, they fear being exposed as a fraud.

There's also a cultural component to consider; in some cultures, speaking highly of oneself is seen as boasting, which can be socially frowned upon. This cultural belief can influence women's willingness to engage in self-promotion, especially in multicultural workplaces.

Despite these obstacles, self-promotion is a critical skill for career advancement and leadership presence. It requires a balanced approach that aligns with one's values, leverages the right platforms, and focuses on sharing successes in a way that also celebrates the team's effort. The goal is to normalize self-promotion as a healthy part of professional life for women, shifting the narrative to one where women can proudly and rightfully claim their achievements without hesitation.

Self-improvement for some women often translates into a relentless pursuit of perfection. There's an ingrained belief that to succeed, one must not only match but exceed the standards often set by male predecessors or counterparts in similar roles—every single time. This drive, although admirable, can morph into an endless quest where "good enough" rarely is, and the goal posts of achievement keep moving. This pressure to continuously enhance skills and knowledge while striving for flawlessness can create an exhausting cycle of self-imposed expectations.

For women, the journey of self-improvement should be reframed from a race toward an unattainable ideal of perfection to a journey of growth that values progress over perfection. It's about recognizing the merit in each step of your personal and professional development, celebrating your small victories, and understanding that making mistakes is a natural part of your learning process. It's about recognizing that true self-improvement isn't about reaching a pinnacle of perfection, but about continuously growing, learning, and contributing in meaningful ways, without the overshadowing pressure to be flawless.

As you navigate the landscapes of leadership, remember: your approach to these topics directly influences your look of leadership. Your appearance isn't merely about the clothes you wear; it embodies the confidence with which you share your accomplishments and the grace with which you pursue personal growth. It's in the assured way you carry yourself, knowing you've earned your place at the table, and in the mindful choices you make that reflect not a pursuit of perfection, but a commitment to continuous improvement. It's about the care you put into yourself and the awareness that you deserve it.

Your look of leadership is a visible extension of where you stand on your journey. Let it be an armor of empowerment, woven with threads of your personal narrative of success and resilience.

This look—your look—of leadership isn't static. It evolves as you do, shaped by every choice that rightfully positions you as an expert in your field and every step of self-improvement that keeps you dynamic and forward-thinking. It's a look that respects where you've been and anticipates where you'll go, all while asserting the undeniable impact you make every single day.

Be Prepared for the Predictable and the Unpredictable

In a world teeming with uncertainty and constant change, the preparedness to face both the predictable and the unpredictable becomes a defining trait of effective leadership. As you stand at the nexus of daily challenges and dynamic shifts, the ability to anticipate and adapt is essential. Hence, your look of leadership should be curated not just for aesthetic appeal but for its strategic function. Curating it with intention is an exercise in scenario planning, a rehearsal for the diverse roles you must play to align the tangible elements of your look of leadership with the intangible dynamics of your day.

Embarking on this sartorial strategy requires contemplation—a series of reflective questions that may guide your choices and ensure your visual presentation is congruent with your professional objectives. Consider, for example, the following:

- What's the big picture for today?
- What's the occasion?
- With whom will you be interacting?
- What will they be wearing?
- What will your client be wearing?
- What will your audience be wearing?
- What will your boss be wearing?
- What will your colleagues be wearing?
- What will your team members be wearing?
- Where are you going to meet?
- Where are you possibly heading after you've met?

- How will you get there?
- Who else could you randomly meet today?
- Which message do you have to deliver today?

Although questions are universally relevant to professionals across the board, as a woman in leadership, there are some additional layers to consider. With this in mind, here are some additional question you might ask yourself:

- How does my attire empower me in spaces where women are underrepresented?
- Does my outfit align with my leadership style while challenging traditional gender norms?
- How does my attire today honor my personal brand and the narrative I wish to convey as a woman in leadership?
- How does this attire serve as a model for other women in my organization striving to define their own professional identity?
- In what ways can I use my attire to make a statement about the inclusivity and diversity values I champion as a leader?
- Can my attire choices today inspire confidence in other women looking to break glass ceilings within the industry?
- How might my clothing choices today mitigate bias or change perceptions about women's roles in leadership?
- How can I use my attire to demonstrate that femininity and professionalism are not mutually exclusive in leadership roles?

The answers to these questions form the cornerstone of your professional presentation. They guide you to select a look of leadership that not only matches the situations you'll face but also allows you to shine in your leadership role—demonstrating intention and preparedness.

By strategically planning, you're taking command of an element of your career that's too often left to happenstance. This proactive approach is a vital step in crafting an image of leadership that communicates you are just as formidable in your appearance as you are in your professional skill set. It's an intentional choice, the armor of a leader poised to tackle the day's challenges.

It's Not Only about Clothes

Yes, looking the part is merely the opening act. It's true that a polished appearance can open doors and instill confidence, but it's the substance behind the style that truly defines a leader. Remember that it's not only about the clothes you wear; it also revolves around embodying the values and responsibilities of your role through every aspect of your professional identity. Your visual appearance might introduce you, but your behavior tells the story of who you truly are. Your communication underscores your competence and empathy, your digital footprint extends your influence beyond the physical walls of any organization, and your environment reflects your professional standards.

BEHAVIOR: Across the dynamic arenas of various organizations, your behavior carries as much weight as your appearance, if not more. The way you conduct yourself—your actions, reactions, and interactions—becomes a living testament to your leadership and professionalism. Consider this: you may dress impeccably, with every detail curated to convey authority, but if your behavior does not align with this presentation, your appearance becomes an empty shell. In the daily demands of leadership, where challenges and opportunities often coincide, your behavior is a guiding light for your team members. It should embody the virtues your look of leadership suggests.

Your behavior also extends to how you handle the unexpected. In any sector, crises are not a matter of if but when.

You might find yourself navigating a critical negotiation, where your leadership and decisiveness are crucial. Here, your composed demeanor amidst adversity, your clear directives, and your swift decision-making reflect the respect and control suggested by your polished appearance. You must be the steady presence in times of tumult, the clarity in times of uncertainty, and the empathy in every strategic decision you make. Let your behavior be the complement to your look of leadership, not a contradiction—and vice versa.

COMMUNICATION: Effective communication in leadership is a nuanced art. It's not merely what you say; it's how you say it. Your tone, your choice of words, and the clarity with which you express complex ideas can alleviate stress or, if mishandled, exacerbate it. Think of it this way: your visual appearance opens the door, but your communication invites people in, offering them a seat at the table in an otherwise challenging environment. Imagine you're presenting a strategic plan. Your crisp look of leadership sets a professional tone, but it's your persuasive communication that will be remembered. You choose words that inspire, not just inform. You explain; you don't just direct. You listen—truly listen—not only to respond but also to understand and to connect.

In these critical moments, your ability to communicate with compassion and clarity can make all the difference in how your leadership is perceived. Your communication is the audible manifestation of your leadership. It's a vital component that, when in harmony with your appearance, establishes you as a leader who is not only seen but heard and understood.

DIGITAL PRESENCE: Your digital presence is, as you know, also a reflection of your reputation, your expertise, and your judgment. This digital reflection of you can either strengthen trust in your professional capabilities or raise doubts about your fitness as a leader.

As you navigate the complexities of your digital presence, it's also essential to consider the emotional contexts in which your online persona might be scrutinized. Your digital footprint is not limited to traditional working hours. It's conceivable that while you're leading a meeting, those you aim to influence are looking you up online, possibly right there in the boardroom or during a break. They might come across your digital interactions, and this could shape their emotional response before they even engage with you. Furthermore, in an era where remote work and virtual collaborations are commonplace, the limitations of digital communication become more pronounced. The nuances of body language, the subtleties of facial expressions, and the inflections of your voice are often diminished or distorted through a screen.

Your digital professional identity should not merely be a shadow of your in-person identity; it should be its affirmation. You need to ensure consistency between your online presence and your physical presence to fortify your leadership narrative. This congruence in identity is crucial; it reassures and confirms to others that the leader they encounter online is the same one leading the charge in the boardroom or the community.

ENVIRONMENT: The choices you make, from the car you drive to the books on your office shelves, all contribute to the tapestry of your professional identity. Each decision, even if seemingly unrelated to your professional responsibilities, can nevertheless color the perception others have of you and that they may leverage, particularly in emotionally charged situations. Consider, for instance, the vehicle you choose; it's not merely a means of transportation but a reflection of your values. An older, poorly maintained car might inadvertently convey to team members a disregard for modern efficiency, potentially fostering doubts about your organizational skills or resource management. Conversely, a luxury sports car might lead to assumptions of extravagance, which could cause clients or colleagues to question your financial judgment.

It's these nuanced, emotional judgments that could reinforce preexisting notions, particularly in moments where trust and leadership are most crucial.

Think also of the people you associate with—friends, family, colleagues. Their appearance, behavior, communication, and digital presence can reflect on you, positively or negatively. You may be judged by the company you keep, so it's prudent to surround yourself with individuals who support and amplify your professional identity.

Every aspect of your life contributes to the overarching narrative of who you are as a woman in leadership and how the assumptions of others either support or challenge you in your leadership journey. The situations you navigate may differ, but the emotional undercurrents of judgment and perception are universal, influencing how you are seen and understood in your role.

Chapter 8
Leadership in a Digital Landscape

The More You Share, the More They Discover.
The Less You Share, the More Suspicion You Invite.

Chapter 8:
Leadership in a Digital Landscape

In the vast expanse of the digital landscape, the rules of leadership presentation have undergone a seismic shift. The advent of the internet, followed by the ubiquity of social media and the increase of virtual encounters, has redefined the parameters. For leaders across all fields, the pivot from a primarily physical presence to a digital one is not just a transition; it's a transformation that requires a savvy understanding of how to navigate this new virtual territory.

Gone are the days when the measure of a woman in leadership was taken first and foremost by a sophisticated look, through a firm handshake, or a direct look in the eye. Today, it's the digital handshake—be it a LinkedIn profile, a professional bio on a company website, a glance through a webcam, or an introductory email—that often precedes any physical meeting. This digital first encounter can be influential enough to impact decisions and perceptions long before a face-to-face interaction.

The digital portrait of a leader must now be as meticulously crafted as their physical presentation. A hastily composed profile, a poorly chosen profile picture, or an unprofessional post can significantly impact one's professional reputation. In this world, search engines act as the new background check, and your online identity speaks volumes, setting the stage for all future interactions. In this age, it's the digital breadcrumb trail that leads others to your professional doorstep—or doesn't.

It forms the narrative of who you are, what you represent, and how you conduct your professional life. A well-managed digital presence can open doors and establish a narrative of expertise and trustworthiness. Neglect it, and you may find that the narrative is written without your consent, shaped by others' interpretations and the whims of algorithms. The stakes are high. A leader's digital presence can be the deciding factor in a client's choice, the turning point in a potential team member's decision to join your ranks, or the catalyst for a partnership that propels your organization forward.

It has the power to bolster or undermine the hard-earned emblems of your professional identity and standing. As such, it's imperative you not only adapt to this digital evolution but also embrace it with the same level of precision and dedication you would apply to any professional endeavor.

Pause and reflect on the intentional echoes your online actions create. In the digital realm, every click, post, and email contributes to the intentional aspect of your digital footprint. This footprint is a carefully crafted mosaic, each piece a deliberate action adding up to the sum of your online presence. The photograph you choose for professional networking sites, the insightful articles you publish on industry trends, the supportive comments you leave on forums—these are the brushstrokes of your intentional digital presence.

Think about the subtle, unintentional ripples your digital presence may be sending. Because there's a counterpart to this explicit storytelling: your unintentional digital footprint. It's the digital equivalent of body language—the subconscious cues that speak volumes without uttering a single word. This footprint includes the regularity with which you engage online. Are your contributions sporadic or consistent? Do you engage in real-time discourse, or does your digital silence linger long after the conversation has moved on?

The state of your professional profiles and website also whispers secrets about your attention to detail and relevance in a rapidly evolving professional landscape. A profile with outdated information or a professional website with broken links can inadvertently suggest a disconnection from current trends and technologies. Your tech-savviness—or lack thereof—is apparent in the way you navigate digital tools and platforms. Do you leverage the latest features to enhance your service offering, or do you falter with the basics of digital communication? And let's not forget the omnipotent algorithms of search engines. Your visibility or absence on the first page of Google search results can significantly affect your perceived credibility and authority, delineating a picture of prominence or obscurity.

In any profession, where trust and expertise are the cornerstones of leadership, both the intentional and unintentional aspects of your digital footprint must be carefully curated. The silent symphony of actions and inactions forms the backdrop against which your explicit digital engagements are set. It's the combination of the overt and the subtle that collectively composes the full digital score of a leader's online presence.

KNOW: Assessing the Scope of Your e-Shadow

The first step in managing your digital footprint is simply to know and understand what's currently out there about you. This initial phase requires a comprehensive analysis of your online presence and utilizing search engines and social media platforms to get an unfiltered view of how you appear to the outside world.

Engage in a methodical search of your name, including the most common typos, and your titles, supplemented by your industry, the name of your organization, or the sectors you're connected with, spanning across all search engines such as Google, Bing, and Yahoo to ensure thoroughness.

This step exposes the full scope of your online presence, revealing everything from professional milestones to personal moments that have found their way onto the digital stage.

To gain an unfiltered perspective of how the digital world perceives you, use incognito or private browsing modes, features available in most web browsers. This approach removes the personalization of search results, offering a clear, unbiased view of your digital footprint as it would be seen by someone encountering you for the first time online.

This step ensures you're not merely seeing a reflection shaped by your own online behavior but rather the raw image that's presented to the wider world.

Then proceed with an audit of your social media platforms. Begin with a critical assessment of your profile, profile pictures, and header images across platforms. These visual elements serve as the digital front of your persona; they often make the first impression online—before a word about you is read. Ensure these images are not only professionally appropriate but also convey a sense of your commitment to your field, whether through imagery that resonates with your sector or a simple, dignified portrait that speaks of competence and trust.

Next, examine your handles and bio descriptions, as well as the content you've shared. This includes posts, articles, comments, and even likes. Each piece of content should align with your professional values, highlighting your knowledge, dedication to your work, and engagement with the broader community of your industry. It's about more than just steering clear of potential pitfalls such as controversial statements; it's about actively contributing to discussions and sharing insights that affirm your position as a thought leader and a reliable professional.

Equally crucial is the scrutiny of your connections. Remember, the company you keep can impact perceptions of your professional judgment and affiliations. This is just as true online. Ensure your network includes only trusted friends and colleagues, industry leaders, and organizations that hold respect within your sector.

This not only bolsters your professional identity but also cultivates your feed with pertinent, current information, keeping you informed about the latest developments in your field.

Continue with your virtual meetings setup. For professionals today, these digital gatherings are not just a matter of convenience but a critical component of business operations and team coordination. As such, ensuring a professional appearance and environment during virtual meetings is just as crucial as in-person interactions. Consider the visual backdrop of your virtual meetings. A distracting background can detract from the meeting's focus and diminish your perceived professionalism. Poor lighting can make it difficult for others to see you clearly, making communication less effective and potentially impacting the connection you're trying to establish. Audio quality is another critical aspect. Background noise can disrupt the flow of conversation and hinder clear communication. Use a high-quality microphone and consider wearing headphones to minimize external noise.

In the digital era, written communication forms the backbone of daily interactions. Beyond emails and text messages, professionals engage in a myriad of digital correspondences, including project management tools, client portals, professional forums, and even comments on relevant online articles or blogs. Each platform and message carries the weight of your professional identity and requires careful consideration.

And always keep in mind that in the interconnected world of digital communication, the reach and permanence of your clicks and words extend far beyond the immediate recipient. Professionals, entrusted with confidential information or representing their brands, must be especially vigilant. The potential for communications to travel unexpectedly is ever-present.

Emails can easily be forwarded, and a message crafted for a specific individual or group can quickly find its way into unintended inboxes. Social media posts, despite the illusion of control through privacy settings or the ability to delete them, carry the risk of being screenshotted and shared.

Once something is shared publicly, or even with a restricted audience, there's no guarantee against the content being captured and redistributed by others. Even virtual meetings have the risk of being recorded without explicit consent. Third-party tools can capture audio and visual feeds, making any shared information, casual remarks, or discussions vulnerable to unauthorized distribution.

REPAIR: Correcting Your Cyber Image

This stage involves taking active steps to rectify or mitigate any negative aspects of your online presence—the "obvious problems." Whether it's unflattering comments, outdated images, misleading information, or more serious issues like unfounded allegations or the unauthorized release of information, taking decisive action is essential for maintaining your professional integrity.

When negative content is within your control, such as on your personal or professional social media profiles, websites, or blogs, addressing these issues can be relatively straightforward. This could mean removing or editing the content in question or updating profile details to better reflect your current professional standing.

The challenge becomes greater when the adverse content resides on platforms or websites outside of your direct control. In these instances, the initial step is to contact the administrators or content creators, politely requesting the removal or correction of the content. Be clear about the content's negative impact on your professional identity.

If direct requests are unsuccessful, or if the content's removal is complex, it might be wise to engage reputation management professionals. These experts are skilled in strategies to de-emphasize negative content in search engine results, making it less visible or discoverable by those searching for you online.

During this phase, you should also confront the not-so-obvious problems. These are instances where the search results about you are not outright negative, but they don't adequately showcase your achievements or expertise or the positive characteristics you wish to project. A search result that isn't damaging but also fails to showcase your qualifications or contributions to your field can be equally limiting.

The strategy is twofold: enhancement and creation. Start by enhancing existing content. This may involve contacting administrators or content creators to suggest updates or additions that more accurately represent your professional achievements.

At the same time, focus on creating new content that truly reflects your professional identity. This can include publishing articles on reputable industry blogs, participating in interviews or podcasts pertinent to your area of expertise, or engaging in community initiatives that garner positive attention. Using social media platforms to share insights, joining professional discussions, and highlighting your contributions can also greatly enrich the quality of your digital footprint.

Shaping the narrative around your digital presence is essential. Not only does it ensure your online persona accurately reflects your real-world skills and values, but also it establishes you as a thought leader in your field. This proactive stance ensures that when clients, colleagues, or potential partners search for you online, they encounter a comprehensive and affirmative portrayal of your professional identity.

OWN: Claiming Your Virtual Real Estate

To address a potential problem, owning your name online is not just a matter of personal branding; it's a strategic necessity. A potential challenge arises when individuals share your name, a scenario not uncommon. From celebrities dominating search engine results to name twins with a more active online presence, these situations can dilute your digital identity, making it harder for clients, business partners, or industry peers to find the real you.

To tackle this, it's crucial to establish a distinctive online presence that clearly identifies you. This could involve using your middle name or initials in your professional profiles, incorporating professional titles or credentials, or choosing a unique version of your name that's linked to your area of expertise.

These tweaks help ensure that searches for your name lead to you, not someone else. Additionally, this acts as a safeguard against future issues. The ever-changing nature of the internet means new figures can become prominent suddenly, potentially eclipsing your online presence.

For example, if a new celebrity with your name emerges, they could take over search results. Or worse, someone with a negative reputation could impact the perception of your shared name. Establishing a clear and unique online identity reduces these risks, keeping your professional achievements and reputation front and center.

This means going beyond merely setting up profiles on popular platforms such as LinkedIn or Instagram. It involves a comprehensive approach to claiming your name across all digital channels, ensuring that you, and only you, control how your name is represented online.

The process begins with registering your name on as many social media platforms, professional directories, and relevant online forums as possible. Although it might seem daunting to maintain active profiles on each, the goal isn't necessarily to be active everywhere but to prevent others from assuming your identity or diluting your online presence. By owning your name on these platforms, you create a protective barrier around your digital identity, making it harder for others to impersonate you or misrepresent your professional brand.

Furthermore, secure your domain name (e.g., YourName.com). Even if a personal website is not in your immediate plans, having your domain is a crucial part of digital ownership.

It blocks others from capitalizing on your name and sets the stage for a centralized space for your professional portfolio and contributions.

Also, delve into niche platforms and professional directories tailored to your industry. These channels enable you to claim your name in more specialized areas and improve your visibility amongst peers, acting as further validation of your professional identity and solidifying your standing within your professional community.

By taking these steps, you ensure that when you are searched for online, you present a consistent and controlled narrative, showcasing the breadth of your professional life, visible not only to clients or team members but also the wider industry network.

CONTROL: Commanding Your Digital Boundaries

Taking control in the digital realm extends beyond just owning your name across various platforms; it's also about meticulously managing the nuances of your online presence.

First, examine the privacy settings on all your social media profiles. Each platform offers a range of options that control who can see your posts, who can tag you, who can comment on or share your content, and even who can send you friend requests or follow you. It's essential to tailor these settings to suit your personal preferences and professional needs, ensuring your content is visible to the right audience while protecting your privacy.

Also consider the implications of your current connections because they can reflect on your professional persona. Be mindful of whom you accept or seek out because these connections can be viewed as an endorsement of your professional standards and network.

Moreover, be proactive in managing the content associated with your profile. Regularly review tags and mentions, removing or disassociating yourself from any content that doesn't align with your professional identity or privacy preferences.

This might include untagging yourself from photos or asking colleagues to refrain from mentioning you in certain posts.

Additionally, think about the visibility of your likes, comments, and shares. These actions can be as telling as the content you post directly.

They contribute to the overall narrative of your professional persona online, so it's wise to conduct these interactions with the same care and consideration you'd give to your own posts.

Finally, keep abreast of updates to privacy policies and settings on each platform. Social media sites frequently update their privacy features, and staying informed allows you to adjust your settings proactively, ensuring continuous control over your digital presence.

By taking these steps, you not only protect your professional reputation but also establish boundaries that respect your privacy and the privacy of those you interact with online. In an era where digital interactions can have real-world implications, such control is not just advisable—it's indispensable.

MONITOR: Persistent Surveillance of Your Online Self

The final step in managing your digital footprint is to vigilantly monitor your online presence. Regularly checking how you appear on the internet isn't an act of vanity; it's a critical component of professional reputation management. There's no harm and no shame in frequently searching for your name in search engines.

One effective strategy is to set up automated alerts. Most search engines offer this feature for free, sending you notifications whenever your name appears online. This proactive approach ensures you're always informed about your digital mentions, allowing you to address any new content quickly.

If you work in an industry where client reviews and testimonials are common across search engines, social media platforms, general review sites, or industry-specific platforms, make sure to consistently review those too.

Publicly expressing gratitude for positive feedback not only reinforces the favorable aspects of your services but also motivates others to share their experiences.

Addressing negative comments is equally critical. Prompt and constructive responses to less favorable reviews demonstrate your commitment to valuing client input and to service improvement.

This approach is a chance to transform a challenging situation into a testament to your dedication to client satisfaction and service excellence.

In the fast-paced digital world, narratives can quickly spiral out of control if not addressed promptly. Being aware of what's being said about you online allows you to take timely action, whether it's correcting inaccuracies, responding to feedback, or updating your digital content to better reflect your professional identity.

And while it straddles a fine line in terms of privacy, keeping an eye on the digital activities of your team members can also be prudent.

Whether it's through email communication, virtual meetings, or interactions on various digital platforms, each digital touchpoint offers an opportunity for you to reinforce your professional identity. It's not enough to curate a strong social media presence or a polished professional website; every digital interaction must be approached with the same level of care and strategic thinking. This holistic approach to managing your digital identity not only safeguards your professional reputation but also amplifies the positive impact you can have within your field.

Your look of leadership knows no bounds, it resonates through every pixel and screen and extends beyond the confines of your office walls, casting a digital silhouette as vast as your ambition.

Chapter 9
Leaders Lead by Example

By Changing Nothing,
Nothing Changes.

Chapter 9: Leaders Lead by Example

Your most paramount duty in your leadership role is not just to lead; it's also about cultivating more leaders—by demonstrating that exceptional leadership is less about dictating actions and more about setting a compelling example. By embodying the values and standards you wish to see, you become a leader others are inspired to follow. This approach is what distinguishes a true leader from a mere manager. Whereas managers focus on ensuring tasks are completed, issuing directives, and adhering to the letter of the law, leaders inspire action through their own choices. They don't just tell their team what to do; they show them how it's done. Your actions send a powerful message of "Do as I do," fostering an environment of mutual respect and emulation.

Great leaders intuitively understand that leading by example is the most potent form of guidance that creates an unspoken standard: an organic dress code, a blueprint for behavior, a benchmark for communication, a template for digital engagement, and a standard for the living and nonliving elements that you surround yourself with in your environment that is far more influential than any written policy.

Your team members and colleagues are always observing, learning, and, in many cases, emulating your actions. Being a leader means accepting that you're always on stage, setting an example for every person you interact with. And although it might sound obvious, every moment of the day it's crucial, then, to ensure the example you're setting is a positive one.

By practicing what you preach and paying attention to the minutiae of your professional identity, you not only enhance your leadership but also inspire your team to strive for the same excellence. The flip side, being a poor role model, is the easiest way to undermine your own authority as a leader. Does that mean you have to follow all the rules (and burdens) your organization puts on you? Maybe. Does that mean you can't have your own style and can't stand out and show your personality? Absolutely not.

Influential leaders are confident, and they trust themselves enough to live their own interpretation of a professional identity. They've put so much thought into it and created such a defined professional identity that their presence is instantly felt when they walk into the room. They're mindful of how others could perceive them and of how they want to be perceived by others.

If part of this leadership image building requires women to wear denims, they wear denims. If wearing sneakers with their suit adds something unique to their defined professional identity, they wear sneakers. Influential women exude confidence and trust in their ability to craft a distinct professional identity that resonates with who they are.

Courageous women don't make excuses. They apologize when they've done something wrong. And usually people have the most respect for those who don't hesitate to say, "I'm sorry," or simply "I was wrong." But people have a hard time respecting those who look for excuses in advance. A leader makes commitments, not excuses. If team members see commitment, courage, and taking responsibility for the actions and choices leaders have made, it feels safe and right to them to follow that person.

And the same is true for your team members. When it comes to their visual representation, you too might be faced with a variety of excuses. Sometimes they claim it's too hot or too cold to dress appropriately, letting the climate dictate their professional standards. Financial concerns also play a role, with some feeling the pinch of investing in high-quality wardrobe items, worrying about the cost or also grappling with guilt over spending.

Time, that ever-elusive commodity, is another barrier, with the hustle of daily life supposedly leaving little room for meticulous planning. Amid these justifications, a deeper thread of resistance emerges. A claimed lack of style sense becomes a shield against change, and the actions of other team members—"They do it too"—serve as misguided validation. Geographic excuses, such as the claim "We're in the suburbs, not Manhattan," highlight a misunderstanding that professionalism has a zip code. Venturing into the digital realm, some diminish the importance of a polished online presence with a wave of the hand, dismissing it as "just the Internet." This underestimation overlooks the profound impact of digital impressions in today's interconnected world.

These excuses, although varied, share a common theme: they believe that professionalism is confined to a specific weather forecast, price tag, or zip code. As a woman in leadership you might find yourself entangled in a web of excuses; and these justifications echo through the corridors, whispered by team members at all levels. They observe their colleagues seeking loopholes in the standards that might justify their choices.

In this landscape of justifications and rationalizations, your role as a leader becomes crucial. Successful leaders sidestep these excuses to send a clear message to their team members: professionalism is nonnegotiable, integral to the fabric of the organization, and essential for individual and collective success.

The Leader's Challenge: It's Not You, It's Someone Else

Sending a clear message to team members sometimes means having honest conversations with your team about sensitive topics that can range from inappropriate clothing to personal hygiene issues, from mismanagement of emotions to unfortunate social media posts, from neglecting workspaces to disrespecting stakeholders. Although these discussions may feel uncomfortable, they're integral to maintaining the professional integrity your role demands.

And it's not uncommon for leaders to feel apprehensive about raising such subjects. Do you? Maybe it's because of . . .

- Your commitment to fostering a positive team environment, knowing harmony is pivotal to operational success.

- An inclination to avoid causing emotional distress given your role, which may be centered on support and development.

- Concern over possible adverse reactions that could disrupt team cohesion.

- The need to exercise authority while maintaining a non-confrontational stance to preserve a cooperative team spirit.

- A tendency to avoid uncomfortable situations, particularly in a setting where team members work closely and collaboratively.

- Finding the right words to express your concerns can be challenging.

- Thinking you are entering a personal space by addressing these issues.

However, remember that first and foremost, your goal is to support your team members' professional development, not to criticize them personally.

Here's how you can approach these delicate conversations with confidence and clarity:

Begin by thoroughly preparing for the discussion. It's crucial to enter these conversations with a clear understanding of the issue at hand. Start by identifying the problem with precision. Reflect on the consequences this problem creates, not just for the individual involved but for the entire team, clients, and the organization as a whole. If it doesn't affect anyone, there's no need for a conversation, after all.

Determine who is directly responsible for the issue. It's essential to pinpoint when the issue first arose and assess its frequency. Reflect on previous attempts to address the problem and their outcomes. This preparation helps you approach the conversation with a solid foundation, making it easier to discuss potential solutions effectively.

Finally, assess whether this is a conversation you should have independently or if it would benefit from the presence of another party, such as a human resources representative or a senior colleague. This decision should be based on the nature of the issue, its sensitivity, and the potential impact on the individual or team.

Get guidance before you approach. In any case, it's recommended you consult with human resources or a legal advisor if you have access to such a source, because some issues carry legal implications and require a delicate approach. Before diving into conversations about sensitive topics such as alcohol, drugs, religion, sex, violence, theft, fraud, harassment, or bullying, it's wise to consult with an expert. These experts can provide essential guidance on handling the situation correctly, inform you about any disciplinary actions that may be appropriate, and ensure you adhere to laws and policies.

Seeking such advice serves as a protective measure for both you and your organization. It helps prevent potential missteps that could lead to false accusations or lawsuits. Addressing such matters without proper preparation and understanding of the legal context could inadvertently cause significant harm.

Pick the best time and space. Selecting the appropriate setting for such a delicate conversation is critical, especially within the bustling environment of corporate offices or similar settings. These kinds of conversations should never occur in public spaces like hallways, where there's a risk of being overheard or observed by others, compromising the privacy and dignity of the team member involved. Instead, opt for a quiet, private space where confidentiality can be maintained—perhaps your office or a secluded meeting room. This environment ensures both you and the team member feel secure, don't get distracted, and are able to speak openly without fear of interruptions.

Additionally, choosing the right moment can significantly impact the receptiveness and outcome of the discussion. Avoid scheduling these talks during peak operational hours or just before or after stressful meetings, because stress levels and distractions can hinder the effectiveness of your message. Instead, find a time when both you and the team member are least likely to be under immediate pressure, allowing for a more focused and constructive exchange. You don't want to have to rush through this conversation because doing so could lead to misunderstandings or the feeling that the issue isn't really being taken seriously.

Bring yourself into the right mindset. Remember that these conversations are not personal attacks against your team member. Instead, they're meant to be constructive and help your team member, team, and organization improve. Remember that neither of you is looking forward to this conversation. It's likely your team member is just as anxious as you are. So take a few minutes to clear your head and remind yourself of that objective.

Start the conversation with positive reinforcement. This instantly reaffirms the value of your team member, especially if you share praise about measurable achievements. This could include citing specific instances in which their attention to detail improved project outcomes, their quick thinking averted a potential crisis, or their insights led to a significant reduction of costs.

Conversely, vague compliments like "You're doing great" or "We appreciate your hard work" lack the specificity needed to make the individual feel genuinely recognized. Such statements fail to highlight the unique contributions of the team member and can turn against you: "Well, you said I'm doing great. So what's the point?" Focusing on concrete achievements sets a constructive tone, demonstrating you value their contributions in a specific area while allowing there is room for improvement in another.

Use neutral and straightforward language. It's crucial to be clear and precise to ensure there's no room for misunderstanding. For instance, instead of saying, "Your outfits are inappropriate," you need to specify, "I've noticed that your wardrobe choices, particularly in during client interactions, may not align with our company's expectations. This is especially true when you wear xyz." This approach makes your feedback not only more actionable but also less personal and more focused on professional standards. Aim for a delivery that is straightforward and unembellished, yet sensitive. Let the facts speak for themselves, and calmly present them without the distortion of emotional undercurrents. This ensures feedback is received as intended: as a means to maintain professional standards and uphold the company's reputation, rather than as a personal critique.

Don't refer to others. When you address a concern with a team member, center the conversation on your own observations rather than on third-party comments or hearsays. It's crucial to base your conversation on incidents you've witnessed personally, not on anecdotes or grievances passed on by others. If the situation occurred in your absence or cannot be personally verified, it's vital to have written, verifiable evidence to substantiate your points. This approach not only preserves the dignity of your team but also strengthens the trust between you and them.

Describe the consequences for them and your organization. Articulate the impact on their own reputation and the broader impact of their actions. For instance, explain how their choices not only hamper their own professional growth but also tarnish the collective reputation of the team, department, and organization. This perspective shift helps the team member understand the gravity of the situation beyond their individual sphere. For example, constant tardiness might not only affect their workload but also strain team dynamics and departmental efficiency. However, address these concerns without making it about your personal grievances (i.e., "I" statements). The focus should remain on the consequences of their actions on themselves and the organization, not on you as an individual leader. This ensures the feedback is purposeful and targeted toward fostering an environment in which their own well-being and the highest levels of organizational excellence are maintained.

Be clear about how you would like them to change. Rather than dwell on the past, move quickly on to the future. But don't expect your team member to know exactly what you expect them to change. For instance, if a team member has been inconsistent in meeting project deadlines, don't just highlight past delays. Instead, clearly outline the steps for improvement, such as adhering to a timeline for task completion, providing exact dates, and announcing regular progress updates. Specify that these measures are nonnegotiable for maintaining the high standards of productivity and professionalism your team is committed to. Unless you're specific in your request, there will be confusion about what needs to be done (or not) moving forward.

Be careful when offering support. Although it's essential to be supportive, emphasize that the responsibility for improvement rests with the team member. You should be there to assist, but the obligation is on them. This stance prevents dependency and promotes accountability.

Be prepared for pushback. In fact, anticipate it—it's a natural response. However, it's crucial to maintain your composure and keep the dialogue centered on the matter at hand. Instead of allowing their response to sidetrack the conversation, seize it as a chance to emphasize your expectations and the importance of meeting them. Instead of leaping to defend your stance with rigidity, pause and truly hear what your team member articulates.

Misunderstandings, fear, or frustration often underpin their responses. This attentiveness not only demonstrates respect for their viewpoint but can also diffuse tensions, paving the way for a dialogue that's both more constructive and collaborative.

Although you can acknowledge their emotions as a way to navigate through their initial reactions, seize the moment to once again clarify the issue at hand, the solution you discussed, and the impact it otherwise has. By reiterating the conversation's objective—to foster their development and enhance overall outcomes—you underscore the collective aim of this exchange.

Finally, remember, your conversation is not a personal critique from you, and similarly, their reaction is not a personal attack on you.

Summarize what was discussed and announce a follow-up. As you draw the conversation to a close, it's essential to encapsulate the key points discussed. This summarization isn't just about reiterating the issues at hand but also about confirming the mutual understanding and commitment to the agreed-upon actions. It's a moment to ensure no detail is lost and both parties are aligned in their expectations and responsibilities.

Announcing a follow-up or a check-in at a specific date is the next critical step, one that underscores your dedication to the process, the individual's progress, and the overall success of your organization. However, this promise carries weight only if it's fulfilled. Failing to follow through not only diminishes the effectiveness of the initial conversation but also erodes your authority and credibility.

End the conversation on a neutral note. The way in which such a conversation concludes can significantly influence the subsequent actions and attitudes of your team member. It's essential to strike the right balance in the closing moments, ensuring the team member doesn't leave feeling overly discouraged or burdened by the discussion.

Conversely, ending on an excessively optimistic note might dilute the importance of the feedback you have given, a phenomenon I refer to as "sandwich" feedback: when the critical message is sandwiched between two positives, it potentially lessens its impact. Aim for a neutral closure, such as "Let's go back to work," which signals the discussion is complete and is just one of many interactions you have in your leadership role.

Document the exchange. This ensures there is a clear record, safeguarding both you and your organization against future misunderstandings or disputes regarding performance or conduct.

Start by documenting who was present during the meeting, capturing the full context of the discussion. It's vital to include the date, time, and location to anchor the conversation in a specific moment and place. This level of detail provides a foundation of transparency and accountability for all parties involved.

Next, meticulously record the substance of the meeting. What issues were discussed? This includes the initial observations that prompted the conversation, the feedback you provided, and the team member's response.

Crucially, detail the agreed-upon actions, including who is responsible for what and the timelines for these actions. This clarity prevents any ambiguity about expectations and responsibilities, ensuring everyone is aligned on the path forward.

Furthermore, outline the expected outcomes of these actions. What changes or improvements should result from this intervention? This sets a clear benchmark for assessing progress and effectiveness. Finally, specify the follow-up steps, including who will carry them out and when.

Documenting these aspects creates a comprehensive and indisputable record of the conversation. And this thoroughness underscores the gravity with which you, as a leader, approach your role, demonstrating a commitment to fairness, transparency, and the growth of your team.

There may also be instances when you encounter a situation that falls outside your direct span of authority. Perhaps you're leading a project with team members who don't directly report to you or you're in a matrix organization in which your influence is more lateral than vertical.

In this case, it's not recommended that you have this kind of conversation. Instead, engage with the individual's direct leaders or with those who have the authority, sharing your observations and concerns—in the best case with documentation that underscores your concern. To them, position your feedback not as criticism but as an opportunity for collective improvement, emphasizing the shared mission of providing exceptional care. In these delicate scenarios, your role as a leader is to facilitate positive change indirectly, using your influence to advocate for standards that align with the organization's values and objectives. It's a dance of diplomacy, requiring patience, empathy, and a strategic understanding of organizational dynamics.

As you can see, leadership is a journey filled with challenges and responsibilities. It demands courage to engage in difficult conversations, wisdom to navigate the limitations of your authority, and the vision to see beyond immediate issues toward the greater goal of positive change. Always remember, the true mark of leadership is not just in wielding authority but in inspiring growth, fostering resilience, and leading by example, even—and especially—when the path is complex.

Chapter 10
Moving Forward

If You Think You Can't,
Well Then You Can't.

Chapter 10: Moving Forward

In concluding our journey through leadership and the crafting of your professional identity, it's essential to recognize that enhancing your leadership image is not merely for personal gratification; it is a fundamental aspect of your professional development. This endeavor brings rewards that extend well beyond the surface. It influences trust within your network, team cohesion, and opportunities for career progression. The critical question now shifts from whether you should refine your professional identity to the depth of your commitment to ongoing improvement and the pursuit of excellence. In the dynamic landscape of any industry, where challenges and prospects exist side by side, the need to distinguish oneself for the right reasons is paramount. The capacity to set oneself apart through an outstanding professional identity is what differentiates the true leaders. These leaders establish an identity that aligns with the values and goals of their organizations, meets the expectations of their stakeholders, supports the ambitions of their teams—and, of course, values themselves as the great leaders they are.

This book has aimed to guide you through the nuanced dance of this professional identity, blending the science of first impressions with the art of a sustained imprint. From the subtle cues conveyed by your visual appearance to the profound influence of digital footprints, many aspects of your professional identity have been dissected, offering you a blueprint for intentional self-presentation.

Now, about that potato chip on the cover. Did you notice?

At first glance, it may seem like a whimsical choice for a book dedicated to such a serious topic. Yet it serves as a powerful metaphor for the concept of identity—personal and professional alike.

Imagine, for a moment, we're embarking on a journey together through a bustling supermarket. As we navigate the aisles, our attention is drawn to the myriad of products vying for our attention.

The significance of packaging design becomes strikingly apparent—the strategic placement of brands, the few critical seconds that influence our decision to add an item to our shopping cart. It's in these moments that the familiarity of a trusted brand effortlessly convinces us to make a purchase, whereas the allure of a new product demands our notice through meticulously crafted packaging designed to leave a lasting first impression.

Consider, for a moment, the relationship between a product and its packaging. Although they are often perceived as separate entities, the most impactful packaging designs demonstrate that thoughtful packaging can not only complement but also enhance the product within. The packaging's shape, size, colors, and imagery are all meticulously chosen to sway your decision to buy or pass.

Now, let's pause in front of the snack aisle, and let's stare at the hundreds of potato chip packages in front of us. Chip packaging offers fascinating insights into successful branding. Did you ever realize that every potato chip packaging has an image of a chip on the front? Did you notice how the most successful chip brands manage to communicate a clear promise: "What you see is what you get." The imagery shows perfectly shaped potato chips, which conveys the product's appeal more than any description could. It's straightforward, with no frills, showing the product in its most enticing form.

Yet there's a twist to this tale, as you know. The crumbled reality inside the bag doesn't match the perfection depicted on the outside.

Despite not having a transparent section to preview the contents, we're drawn in by the promise of ideal, unbroken chips. Not just once—again and again we continue to buy them, even if we're aware of the illusion.

The lesson here is profound: a compelling external presentation can lead people to embrace you, even if the internal reality doesn't quite match up (yet). Achieving the opposite effect is significantly more challenging.

For leaders, the metaphor of potato chip packaging is a poignant one for the importance of a consistent professional identity. You must ensure that your external presentation—your appearance, behavior, communication, digital presence, and work environment—reflects you in the best light.

Just as the chip bag's imagery promises a certain experience, leaders must convey an identity that their teams and stakeholders can instantly respect and trust. Although no leader is without flaws—comparable to the mix of whole and broken chips within a bag—it's the strategic depiction of your competencies and commitment that should be emphasized. Over time, just as consumers come to accept the imperfect contents of a chip bag due to their trust in the brand, so too will others accept a leader's human flaws if they are convinced of the leader's dedication to their role and the success of the team.

Now let's take another look at the aisle of potato chips in front of us, and let's contemplate expectations. If I were to ask you to pick a spicy flavor of these chips, you'd likely subconsciously look out for a red bag. An organic variant? Green or brown.

Our brains are wired to associate specific colors and designs with certain product attributes. This principle of expectation extends beyond the supermarket aisle to the realm of leadership. Just as we have predefined notions about product packaging, we harbor expectations about a leader's professional identity.

Despite the diversity in leadership styles and personalities, certain universal expectations remain consistent.

Just as the bold red packaging of spicy chips stands out to a shopper looking for flavor, leaders who align their presentation with professional norms are easily recognized and trusted. There's certainly space for individuality and a break from convention, like a neon-pink chip bag among the typical reds and greens on a shelf. A leader might also choose to deviate from traditional visual cues through distinctive clothing or an unconventional approach. This differentiation can attract attention, drawing those intrigued by novelty and signaling innovation. However, it may also miss the mark of subconscious expectations, posing a challenge to immediate recognition as a leader in their professional field. Much like a shopper instinctively reaching for the familiar red bag, oblivious to a pink option, people often gravitate toward the comfort of what they know—traditional emblems of authority and expertise.

Finally, like well-established potato chip brands that are strategically positioned at eye level on shelves to be easily seen and chosen, influential leaders naturally command a presence and often enjoy higher recognition, similar to products occupying premium shelf space. Conversely, less prominent brands—or leaders—might need to exert more effort to be noticed.

In a competitive professional environment, being at eye level signifies remaining at the forefront of your managers' and all stakeholders' minds, always ready to be selected for your visible dedication to excellence, professionalism, and service. This prominence isn't merely physical; it extends to the entire professional identity you construct as a leader.

As this chapter closes, let the lasting lesson be the craft of your professional identity—the external manifestation of your inner capabilities. Let the professional identity you create stand as your unwavering representative, conveying expertise, fostering trust, and managing the intricacies of leadership with poise.

Your "packaging" is not merely an aesthetic choice; it's a strategic tool that, when aligned with your skills and vision, can weather the storms of challenge and change. Let it amplify your strengths, not overshadow them.

As you move forward, may your professional identity resonate with intention, your leadership echo with impact, and your presence be felt even in silence.

Stand out not just to be seen but to make a difference, to inspire trust, and to drive progress.

Here's to the leader in you—packaged to perfection, poised for greatness, and perpetually ready to turn challenges into opportunities.

Go forth and lead, not just with authority but with the magnetism of a well-crafted identity, one that's as compelling and multifaceted as the leader within you.

Acknowledgments

To you, the reader:

I am in awe of the quiet strength of the unseen women in organizations, the unsung heroines whose contributions are often overlooked—your work does not go unnoticed here. And equally, I celebrate the women top executives who carve pathways for those who follow, who break ceilings so others may rise—your trailblazing sparks the fires of progress.

Thank you to the fearless advocates and champions of equality, for your relentless commitment to breaking down barriers, challenging stereotypes, and paving the way for a more inclusive and equitable world.

To the grandmothers and mothers who have raised daughters to stand tall and sons to stand in solidarity with women—your nurturing has shaped leaders and allies alike. For those of you who may not have experienced motherhood, know that your influence extends deeply, enriching the lives of all the children you encounter with your wisdom and care.

I admire those who were not born as women but have joined this profound sisterhood—your bravery and courage enriches us all. Your journeys shed light on the diversity and inclusivity that strengthen the tapestry of womanhood.

Luckily, there are fathers, brothers, uncles, and all the men in our lives who know they play an essential role in shaping a world where women can thrive. Your support, encouragement, and respect are vital in the journey toward equality.

Same to the men in organizations and beyond, who listen, amplify, and advocate for women's voices, who champion diversity and foster an environment of inclusion—your allyship is powerful and appreciated.

To the daughters and sons, the young people (he/she/they) of today: Know that we have come a long way in the fight for gender equality, but there is still much work to be done. Although we strive to create a world that is fair and inclusive for you, there will inevitably be challenges for you along the way. In these moments, always remember to look out for one another, to support and uplift each other, or to reach out to a woman for guidance.

And finally, my deepest appreciation to the many women who have supported me, challenged me, inspired me, laughed and cried with me, and who have taught and learned with me—your myriad of contributions embroider the fabric of my personal and professional journey.

As you close this book, to each of you, in all the roles you play, remember that your actions forge the future we all share. As you turn the final page, remember that your work and your leadership echo in the legacy you leave, in the communities you uplift, and in the lives you transform.

With the deepest respect and admiration,
Sylvie di Giusto

About the Author

International keynote speaker Sylvie di Giusto brings her expertise from a successful corporate career in Europe to every presentation. Formerly the head of a management academy and innovation hub, she developed innovative leadership programs for high-end education with unprecedented training methods. As the chief of staff for the chief human resources officer of Europe's largest tourism and retail group, Sylvie coordinated all group-wide human resources teams and activities. Prior to that, at a consultancy firm, she implemented online and in-person training and development initiatives for Fortune 100 companies.

Now, extraordinary professionals at respected organizations around the world—including American Express, American Airlines, Hilton, Nespresso, Microsoft, Prudential, and even the US Air Force—trust Sylvie to help them make the right decisions that grow their brands and bottom lines. Building on her five cornerstones of modern emotional intelligence—visual, behavioral, verbal, digital, and social intelligence—Sylvie gives her audiences Power of Choice, a conscious decision-making framework that allows us to understand our perceptions, choose our behaviors, and determine our best outcomes.

Sylvie is the author of *The Image of Leadership, Discover Your Fair Advantage* and the upcoming *Make Me Feel Important*. Sylvie takes audiences on an entertaining, spectacular, and thought-provoking journey through the brain and mind and from the unconscious to the conscious—and ultimately to the heights of personal, professional, and organizational success.

For speaking engagements, contact Sylvie's wonderful team at: sylviebookings@cmispeakers.com, or call +1-403-398-8488.

Perception Audit

Take the free Perception Audit and unveil the image you project to the world in just 15 minutes. Receive a personalized report that illuminates how others perceive your professional identity, and learn to align your self-view with the impression you intend to make.

Are you ready to meet the YOU that everyone else sees?

Or visit sylviedigiusto.com/audit

After you've gained the clarity you need to polish your professional identity and project the very best version of you in the workplace and beyond, let's stay connected! Follow me on social media to join the conversation about *The Image of Leadership for Women*.

- instagram.com/sylviedigiusto
- linkedin.com/in/sylviedigiusto
- facebook.com/sylviedigiusto
- youtube.com/c/sylviedigiusto
- tiktok.com/@sylviedigiusto

Your Voice and Our Collective Reach

Books—just like you—face perception challenges.

In a world where perception is reality, nowadays the value and impact of books are often judged by the quantity and quality of their Amazon reviews. So if this book has offered new perspectives or valuable insights, please consider sharing your experience online. Your review not only helps shape the book's impact but also guides others to find the same resource you did.

Your role in this narrative could just be the beginning.

For those who have found resonance within these pages and wish to spread the wisdom within their team or organization, I offer preferred customer pricing for bulk orders. Please reach out to my wonderful team at sylviebookings@cmispeakers.com, or call +1-403-398-8488. Let's empower more leaders together.

Made in the USA
Middletown, DE
27 July 2024